Alcohol in Ancient Mexico

Henry J. Bruman returning from a journey to Huichol country, village of Mojarres, near Robles, Nayarit, December 16, 1938. (Photo by Bodil Christiansen)

Alcohol in Ancient Mexico

Henry J. Bruman

Foreword by Peter T. Furst

The University of Utah Press

Salt Lake City

Maps by J. Chase Langford

All photographs by Henry J. Bruman unless otherwise noted

2000 01 02 03 04 05 06
5 4 3 2 1

LIBRARY OF CONGRESS CATALOGING-IN-PUBLICATION DATA

Bruman, Henry J.
    Alcohol in Ancient Mexico / Henry J. Bruman ; Foreword by Peter T. Furst.
        p. cm.
    Includes bibliographical references and index.
    ISBN 0-87480-658-5 (hardcover : alk. paper)
    1. Indians of Mexico—Alcohol use. 2. Indians of Mexico—Rites and
ceremonies. 3. Indians of Mexico—Medicine. 4. Fermentation—Mexico—
History. 5. Drinking of alcoholic beverages—Mexico—History. I. Title.
F1219.3.A42 B78 2000
394.1'3'0972—dc21

                                                    99-050946

Contents

Figures

Maps

Foreword

Peter T. Furst

I

Writing this foreword closes a circle that began for me in 1956, when I first met the author of this work. In those preacademic days, I was a feature writer on social science and anthropology topics. During research for an essay on religious freedom and scientific issues involved in the use of peyote by adherents of the Native American Church, I interviewed Henry Bruman in his office in the Department of Geography at UCLA. I had been told by Carl Sauer, the eminent geographer who chaired Bruman's doctoral committee at the University of California, Berkeley, that Bruman did his Ph.D. dissertation on the aboriginal alcoholic drink areas of New Spain and, in the course of his field research, had spent time with the Huichols in the Sierra Madre Occidental in Mexico. Then as now, and for many centuries into the remote past, the Huichols were the preeminent "People of the Peyote." It followed that Bruman might have some useful things to say on the subject.

He did, even though what drew him to the Huichols and their neighbors was not the peyote cactus, *Lophophora williamsii*, but the fermented maize beer the Huichols call *nawá* and other indigenous peoples in northwestern Mexico know as *tesgüino*.

The fermentation of a variety of native plants and the prodigious use of the results have played an indispensable role in Mesoamerican religion, ritual, divination, and curing for many millennia. And yet, prior to 1940, when Bruman presented his dissertation, entitled *Aboriginal Drink Areas in New Spain*, at Berkeley, nowhere among the thousands of books and papers published over the past century on Mesoamerica had there been anything in print like his comprehensive study. Nor has there been anything else until now, although Mexican scholars and others have published singular studies on pulque and some of the other major regional drinks traditionally employed as ritual inebriants.

There is considerable literature, too, on the ethnobotany and ethnology of the far more potent ecstatic-shamanistic Mesoamerican inebriants called, inaccurately, "hallucinogens," including the already mentioned peyote cactus; sacred mushrooms, mostly of the genus *Psilocybe*; the potent seeds of the morning glories *Turbina corymbosa* and *Ipomoea violacea*, the former known to the Aztecs as *ololiuhqui* and to the Yucatec Maya as *xtabentun*; *Nicotiana rustica* tobacco, its solanaceous relatives *Datura* and *Solandra*, and other species to which the indigenous peoples ascribed divine powers.

But, except for Bruman's dissertation and now this fine book, no one had surveyed the entire field of fermentation and brought it together in one comprehensive volume that is as useful and interesting to the generalist in Mesoamerican studies and the interested public as it is to the ethnohistorian, ethnologist, botanist, pharmacologist, or anyone studying Native American religion and ritual. Certainly no one has drawn so exhaustively on the historical and ethnohistoric sources and tested them against the fieldwork and personal observation—often in rugged and isolated regions of even more difficult access in the late 1930s than they are today—of the continued use of fermented beverages, whose history may in some cases date back five or six thousand years to the primitive beginnings of maize agriculture and, in others, millennia earlier still.

Today, doctoral dissertations are easily accessible in one form or another, but when Bruman graduated in 1940, accessibility was limited. And so, until now, his study has remained virtually unknown and unavailable to a wider audience.

I have always believed that it would have been worth publishing just as it was when he first gave it to me to read in 1956. At that time, and until his retirement, he was a member of the Department of Geography at UCLA. I was then writing for *Fortnight*, the biweekly California journal. It was a period when the press and law enforcement circles were much given to ill-informed and unscientific hullabaloo about peyote and its use in the syncretistic, pan-Indian religion incorporated as the Native American Church of North America. Despite ample documentation for its use by Indian people as a visionary sacrament and its nonaddictive and physiologically benign qualities in such studies as Weston La Barre's classic, *The Peyote Cult*, I was earnestly assured by an otherwise perfectly reasonable Hollywood detective that peyote was the "devil's root" (a pejorative right out of the Inquisition in colonial Mexico), every bit as addictive as heroin, and responsible for all manner of sex crimes. I proposed to *Fortnight's* editor that he let me do a story on constitutional as well as scientific issues involved in the ongoing struggle to gain full religious freedom by and for American Indians. He readily agreed. In the course of my research, I called Weston La Barre at Duke University and got some usable quotes. But as a California magazine we wanted a more local angle.

Bruman's comments were indeed enlightening. Unfortunately, they and all the other material I managed to pull together over several weeks for my freedom of religion article went for naught. Before it could be published, *Fortnight* fell victim to economic circumstances and ceased publication, propelling me, after a stint in documentary television, into a career in academic anthropology that has now spanned close to four decades.

II

I didn't see Henry Bruman again until the early nineteen sixties. By that time I was enrolled in the UCLA doctoral program in anthropology. During my fieldwork, I became more and more interested in Huichol art, religion, ritual, and eventually the ethnobotany and ethnology of sacred plant "hallucinogens" and ritual inebriants in Middle and South America. He became a member of my doctoral committee. Ever generous with his time, knowledge, and insights, he proved to be a very fortunate choice indeed.

But there was one frustration in my relations with him over the next several years: his adamant refusal to let the UCLA Latin American Center publish his dissertation.

Every time Johannes Wilbert (the prolific Latin Americanist and Center director) and I approached him, Henry demurred. He had done the research and written it so long ago it needed to be updated, he said, and for that he was too busy. He hoped to go back to it at some later time, but not then. It is all a long time ago, but I remember making one last stab at convincing him during the little party that followed my doctoral orals, my argument being, as ever, the value of his study for Mesoamerican ethnology, ethnobotany, cultural history, and especially religion.

Inclusion of that last item may seem odd, but the use of fermented beverages and sacred plants in aboriginal rituals is well-documented. To mention just one group: the Lacandón Maya of Chiapas. R. Jon McGee and F. Kent Reilly III write in the Summer 1997 issue of the *Journal of Latin American Lore* that "a principal feature of Lacandon ritual life involves the brewing and consumption of the sacred intoxicating beverage *balché*. Because *balché* is spiritually purifying and brings on a transcendental state in which the supplicant can communicate with the gods, the drink is important in the ritual life of Lacandon men."

This observation applies no less to the Huichols, Tepehuanes, Tarahumara, Mixtecs, Zapotecs, Mixe, the many speakers of Nahuatl (the language of the

Aztecs) and its dialects, or any of the other indigenous languages that still survive in modern Mexico. Among the Lacandón Maya, ritual inebriation is still indivisible from religious ceremony and the philosophy and practice of healers and shamans. Bruman's contributions on *balché* are essential for an understanding of this important aspect of the intellectual culture of the Maya.

For Mesoamerican Indians, then, as for their South American cousins, "getting high," by whatever technique, was a means not of escape but of integration with the sacred. The Spanish clergy recognized this from the very beginning, which is why they tried, sometimes with great ruthlessness, to discourage and suppress these ancient "techniques of ecstasy" and spiritual transformation. Their efforts were doomed to failure, of course. As the well-known physician-ethnobotanist Andrew Weil (*The Natural Mind*, 1972, 1986) and psychopharmacologist Ronald K. Siegel (*Intoxication*, 1989) have convincingly argued, the desire to alter one's state of consciousness is a biological imperative very much on a par with the drive for sex or food. Nor, as Siegel has shown, is this limited to humans: it can be found throughout the animal kingdom all the way down to insects. The colonial clergy ultimately had to accept ritual intoxication as the price of conversion and a necessary, if undesirable, part of Christian observances. I use "undesirable" advisedly, because one of the by-products of ritual intoxication has been widespread alcoholism.

The Aztecs must have been well aware of this danger. The sixteenth-century Franciscan chronicler Fray Bernardino de Sahagún learned from his Aztec consultants that pulque was revered as a gift of the gods to humans and a facilitator of direct contact between them, but was strictly forbidden for everyday use. Rather, it was reserved for religious and ritual occasions—a rigidly enforced prohibition from which only the elderly (significantly) were exempt.

Bruman notes that distillation was unknown in the so-called New World before the arrival of the Europeans. Yet fermentation of wild fruits was surely discovered and utilized many millennia before the first attempts at food cultivation, and certainly long before the rise, ca. 1500 B.C., of the Olmecs, Mesoamerica's first agriculture-based civilization. What is interesting—and here Bruman's work is especially valuable—is that there was much regional specialization, with relatively little overlap. Indeed, one of the many values of this study is that the original research dates to 1938 and 1939. At that time, half a century ago, technological, economic, and ideological acculturation, though a fact of life virtually everywhere, was less pervasive. There was also greater isolation between the areas in which one or another fermented beverage predominated, and so there was less crossover from one area to another, even in the use of so basic and universal a staple as maize for the making of beer. Maize, *Zea mays*–whose protection and propagation in Mexico millennia before the European invasion could as easily have been motivated by the quest for beer as for tamales–and the agave, a goddess in her own right, are both found over a broad geographical area in Mexico. Yet the indigenous inhabitants developed their own preferences for one or another favorite fermented beverage, making it possible for Bruman to divide ancient Mesoamerica not just by language and culture areas but by the various alcoholic beverages preferred by local inhabitants.

Needless to say, with modern travel and commerce these boundaries are now more permeable than in the past, but there is also a remarkable stability and persistence. Following Bruman, I too have found the old cultural preferences intact to a remarkable degree, although "foreign" liquors are now sold even in the most isolated indigenous communities. Tequila is now as easily available to the Yucatec Maya as it is to the descendants of the Aztecs in Central Mexico. So is aguardiente, the potent distillate of sugarcane, a plant unknown before the European invasion.

But although *balché* remains the most important ceremonial Maya inebriant in Yucatán, we learn from this study that modern Maya had adapted to the point where they were finding fermented sugarcane juice (as distinct from the distilled aguardiente) to be an acceptable substitute for the traditional honey produced by the stingless native bee—something of a parallel to the report by Lumholtz a century ago that the Tepecano Indians in northwestern Mexico were substituting marijuana for the traditional peyote cactus when the latter was unavailable for ritual inebriation (something no self-respecting Huichol would ever consider).

Because Henry Bruman hails from a tradition that emphasizes the value of baseline ethnography and firsthand observation, respects the ethnohistoric sources, is tireless in locating and citing the literature—no matter how obscure·—and is not afraid of amending old with new data and insights where that is indicated, his work is rich in facts, up-to-date, and unencumbered by the latest theories.

Bruman's study belongs on the shelves of anyone interested in Mesoamerica. But in its appreciation for the ingenuity of the First Americans in finding ways to feed the spirit as well as the body and in its contribution to a little-understood area of study and experience, I want to repeat what I told its author after he so generously gave me a copy of his Ph.D. dissertation more than four decades ago: this is a work that takes the reader on an intellectual journey far beyond its geographical, historical, and even topical boundaries.

Preface

This book began in 1938 when I was admitted to candidacy for the doctorate in geography under Professor Carl O. Sauer at the University of California, Berkeley, and received a one-year Field Fellowship from the Social Science Research Council. During most of the following year, I visited various Mexican Indian tribes, including the Huicholes, the Otomí, the Huaxtec, the Totonac, the Maya, several groups of Nahua speakers, and others as far south and east as El Salvador and Honduras.

I received my degree in 1940, but revision and publication of my dissertation as a book were interrupted by war. After a brief period as an assistant professor of geography at the Pennsylvania State College, some government work in Washington, D.C., and time as a visiting scholar at Harvard, I was appointed in 1945 as an assistant professor at UCLA, my undergraduate alma mater, where I had received an A.B. in chemistry in 1935. Over the years, as opportunities presented themselves, I conducted additional research on Mesoamerican native drinks in libraries and archives in the United States, Latin America, and Europe. Yet, a time for summation, exposition, and interpretation never seemed to arrive. My late friend Jim Parsons, worthy successor to Mr. Sauer as leader of the Berkeley geography department and president of the Association of American Geographers, wrote me once in a jovial vein, "Henry, your dissertation must certainly be the most widely disseminated *unpublished* doctor's dissertation in the history of the Berkeley libraries." Now, in my 86th year, I feel the time has come to publish the gist of what I found.*

*Almost all the field observations were made in the late 1930s, which undoubtedly permitted me to record some traits that have since disappeared with the continuing Mexicanization and Americanization of native life.

Alcohol in Ancient Mexico

Introduction

This book is a first attempt to differentiate drink areas in aboriginal New Spain. Its primary emphasis is on alcoholic intoxicants. Of course the areas I delineate are not absolute; they are synthesized from overlapping regions of individual drinks. Their boundaries are based on the relative importance of the culturally most significant beverages insofar as such information could be obtained from the literature, manuscript sources, and field inquiry. Thus, where necessary I have supplemented this approach with distributional data concerning the raw ingredients themselves—primarily wild plants whose limits are reasonably well known or derivable from a consideration of environmental limitations.

My inquiry concentrates on the lands between the northern limits of the aboriginal use of alcohol, near the Gila River of Arizona, and as far south as the Isthmus of Panama. This great area falls naturally into two parts: (1) a northern part, including most of Mexico as far southeast as the Isthmus of Tehuántepec, with the exception of the lowlands of the Gulf of Mexico, where baking mescal for food and the preparation of mescal wine are basic; and (2) a southern part, in which mescal utilization was aboriginally absent.

This division has a stronger claim to validity than mere convenience. Baked mescal, together with its lesser local equivalent, sotol, is one of the fundamental foods of the whole northern area, and wine made by the fermentation of baked mescal is a similarly important alcoholic beverage. With the coming of agriculture, mescal for food decreased in importance in most areas. Whether mescal wine declined simultaneously in some areas due to the advent of beer from corn or whether it did not assume its full importance until agriculture brought sedentary economies and skills in pottery making are questions to which no solutions have been found. Alcoholic drinks were even made and used by some groups who had no pottery. There was neither agriculture nor pottery in most of the

"Chichimeca" country of north-central Mexico even at the time of the Conquest, yet the hunting and gathering inhabitants of that land made at least three kinds of alcoholic beverages.

Although mescal wine has come down to the present only in the remote mountain fastness of the Tarahumar, a much wider distribution in earlier times is attested by sixteenth- and seventeenth-century chroniclers. Those parts of Mexico in which an early mescal brandy industry developed—the result of the introduction of stills from Europe and Asia in the sixteenth century—may well have had an unbroken tradition of fermenting baked mescal.

Superimposed on the great mescal region are five culture areas, well defined in terms of native alcoholic intoxicants. They are (1) the *northwest cactus area*, in which wines from sahuaro and pitahaya fruit play a dominant role; (2) the *tesgüino area*, characterized by beer from sprouted maize; (3) the nonagricultural *tuna and mesquite area*, in which wines from nopal cactus fruit (tuna) and from mesquite pods are most important; (4) the *pulque area*, in which the fermented sap of the various pulque agaves is the main intoxicant; and (5) the *mescal and jocote area*, where, in addition to the ubiquitous mescal, an important place is assumed by wine made from the jocote ("hog plum"—*Spondias* sp.). (See Map 1.)

I also discuss the various alcoholic drinks of lesser importance in these areas. There was an unexpectedly wide range for cornstalk wine. The prior existence of this beverage provides a partial explanation of the immediate and widespread post-Conquest shift to sugarcane wine (and rum) among the Indians of the moister lowlands, especially among the Huaxtec and Totonac of the Gulf Coast.

Beyond the limits of mescal, to the south and east, the greater complexities of distribution and the lesser amount of available information make a subdivision into valid drink areas as yet impossible, except in the case of Yucatán, for which a well-defined region of wine from fermented honey and *balché* bark can be established. There are also examples in the rest of the area of fermented beverages made from pineapples, chewed or sprouted corn, various palms, bromelias, and hog plums.

In my opinion the salivary impregnation of starchy materials prior to fermentation is a trait of South American provenance that reaches its northernmost aboriginal limits on the mainland among the tribes of Honduras. Further, palm-stem tapping may not be aboriginal north of the Nicaragua depression, and may possibly be a late pre-Conquest introduction into south of the depression from Africa. Finally, a relative of the Old World banana may have existed in the New World aboriginally and may have served as a source for wine.

The great early importance of coconut wine in western Mexico, especially in the neighborhood of Colima, made it necessary to look into the history of this beverage and, by extension, into the general history of the coconut in America.

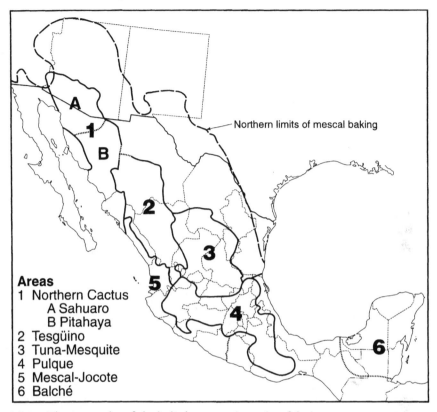

Map 1. The geography of alcoholic beverages in ancient Mexico.

Strong claims have been advanced that the coconut is indigenous to the New World and that it was taken to the Old by trans-Pacific migrants. I do not share these views, but believe that coconuts are native to the general neighborhood of the East Indies; that they came to the Pacific shores of America at a relatively recent time before the Conquest, probably by means of the Equatorial Counter Current and El Niño; and that they established themselves without any intervention on the shores of Panama. Coconut wine was not made in the New World until the Filipino sailors who manned the Manila Galleon introduced it in the late sixteenth century.

The art of distillation was unknown in America aboriginally, but came to Mexico across both oceans in the sixteenth century. With certain modifications, simple Spanish stills were adopted by a number of Indian tribes and by the mestizo population. Filipinos brought with them an even more primitive still having

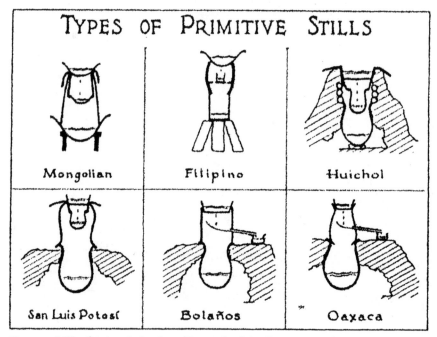

Figure 1. Stills of Asian derivation. (Drawn by John Buoncristiani)

no external receiver that made its way into the barrancas of eastern Nayarit and northern Jalisco, giving rise to the so-called Huichol still. (See Figure 1.)

For those readers interested in the kinds of refinements possible for enhancing intoxicating drinks, Appendix B is a list of auxiliary herbs that were added to native liquors, along with a tentative discussion of their function. A few laboratory tests made on field samples found that many of these herbs have a strong physiological action as a heart stimulant.

ONE

The Non-Alcohol Region
in the North

With one minor exception, no aboriginal alcoholic beverages are definitely known in the New World north of the boundary indicated on Map 1. There was no dearth of fermentable substances, including materials commonly fermented in areas farther to the south. Nor was there a lack in most places of suitable vessels. Mobility was seldom so severe as to interfere seriously with the leisure required in the making of fermented drinks. Yet, such drinks were not made. Quoting Havard:

> We might perhaps account for the ignorance of our eastern Indians concerning "corn beer" which, after all, is only a vile beverage, but we may well wonder at their failure to make wine. To say nothing of our many kinds of berries, more species of grapes grow in this country than in all the rest of the world and, for many tribes, must have been a staple food; again, nothing is easier than to make wine, the process consisting merely in pressing out the juice and letting it ferment. It is strange indeed they should not have stumbled upon it.[1]

An alleged occurrence of aboriginal grape wine is refuted by Payne as follows: "The 'wine' which, according to Barlow (1584), the aborigines of North Carolina made from the wild grape was the fresh juice of the grape boiled with other ingredients."[2]

The one aboriginal exception mentioned above is a case that seems to have no connection with the alcoholic regions to the south and would appear to be explicable only on the basis of such an accidental discovery as Havard had in mind. In 1775, Pedro Fages reported that when the California Indians around San Gabriel Mission were first discovered, they were apparently making a wine out of elderberries.[3]

In other parts of this area the process of fermentation and the use of alcoholic liquor was unknown, except as a dim memory from the south or as the result of late contact with the western outposts of the alcohol users. Among the Iroquois, for example, the tapping of maples, birches, and other trees for their sweet sap was a well-developed activity. They even boiled down the sap to a syrup, although they seem never to have manufactured crystalline sugar.[4] That they should not at some time have allowed some unboiled sap to stand around for a few days until it fermented and then not have tasted it, noticed the new flavor, and experienced the result of imbibing it in quantity is almost inconceivable. Yet, if that event took place it made no impression on the culture of the tribe. Waugh is of the opinion that their backwardness in this connection is ascribable to their lack of receptacles for keeping the beverages. But he mentions that they had earthenware vessels and various other receptacles of bark and wood.[5] With much less satisfactory material equipment the nomadic tribes of the tuna and mesquite region were able to make three different kinds of alcoholic beverages.

Given the great importance of corn in the nutritional picture of the eastern woodlands and the Southwest, it may appear odd that maize beer was unknown north of the Pima. This circumstance is not so surprising as it appears offhand, since the manufacture of such beer by either the chicha or *tesgüino* method is by no means obvious or easily discoverable by accident. Still, the Hopi and the Zuñi made a kind of chewed-corn pudding which, among the Zuñi at least, was sometimes ground, mixed with water, and taken as a beverage.[6] The fermentation of this beverage, accomplished by letting the liquid stand for a few days, would have become a corn chicha reminiscent of the common Central American type. But there is no record that this fermentation was ever allowed to proceed.

The Zúni also came rather close to making *tesgüino*: "A native drink which the Zuñi claim is not intoxicating is made from sprouted corn. The moistened grain is exposed to the sun until it sprouts; water is then poured over it and it is allowed to stand for some days."[7] The procedure is unorthodox in that the corn is left to sprout in the sun instead of in the shade, thus giving rise to green and rather bitter shoots instead of white and sweet ones. The grinding and boiling before fermentation that is necessary for good *tesgüino* is also lacking. There is even a tradition among the Zuñi that they once made a wine from the agave, when they were living in the agave country to the southwest of their present home.[8] It would seem that when the group moved away from the northern end of the *tesgüino* area they radically changed their culture pattern regarding intoxicating drinks. In this regard, they exhibit the typical transitional characteristics of a people peripheral to a culture area. This statement applies also to a number of groups west of the Zuñi, specifically the Southern Paiute, Walapai, Havasupai, Yavapai, and Maricopa (see Table 1, page 26), who make a sweet drink from baked mescal but are not known to ferment it.

The Apache present an involved problem. Their appearance in the Southwest and along the Rio Grande is relatively late, and, with one exception, their alcoholic drinks were borrowed from their new neighbors. They learned how to bake mescal and brew mescal wine[9] and how to make *tesgüino*.[10] For the San Carlos Apache a pitahaya wine is also recorded.[11] The only drink that seems to be peculiarly their own is made from the sweet inner bark of the pine tree. The drink is mentioned only for the Mescalero, who sometimes also mixed it with *tesgüino*. No details of manufacturing are given. Both Mescalero and Jicarilla use the bark also for food by pounding it into a pulp and baking it into cakes.[12] Whether they brought this beverage with them from the north or whether they learned to make it in their new home after they became acquainted with alcoholic drinks from the south is impossible to say. The apparent association of the bark wine with *tesgüino* would lend some weight to the latter view. Most likely it was a case of an old resource turned to a new use through the infiltration of new ideas.[13]

The Concho, Suma-Jumano, Coahuiltec, and Tamaulipec are not known to have had alcoholic beverages aboriginally. At no point does the trait seem to have reached the Rio Grande. The most probable boundary lies a hundred or two hundred miles to the southwest, parallel to the river (see Map 1 and Table 1). Hence, it is probable that the western Apache acquired alcoholic drinks much earlier than the groups to the east.

The very limited penetration of alcoholic beverages into northeastern Mexico as compared to the northwest is impressive. It was the result of four main factors: (1) lack of fixed habitation, (2) lack of pottery, (3) presence of a local intoxicant that made alcohol unnecessay, and (4) effective remoteness from the great culture center of the south-central plateau, where several drink areas met. The last-named reason was undoubtedly the decisive one. In the tuna and mesquite region, the first three also hold true, but, because of better contact with the south, alcoholic beverages played a significant role. We may conjecture that the Chichimeca, who belong to the Otomí linguistic family, especially the Pame, were the intermediaries that transferred the use of alcoholic beverages from their sedentary linguistic kin to the south to their economic kin to the north and west. Further spread of alcoholic beverages toward the north was hampered (1) by a general weakening of the trait due to a somewhat unfavorable environment; (2) by increasing difficulty of cultural interchange due to sparse population, lack of fixed habitation, and diversity of language; and (3) by an increasing importance of the local intoxicant, peyote. In contrast, the spread northward in the *tesgüino* and northwest cactus regions was favored by much better cultural contact due to greater total population, sedentary location, and closely related languages, as well as by the lack of a powerful competitive intoxicant.

The Seri represent a miserable exception in the culture picture of the northern part of the west coast. That they still make pottery would indicate a one-time sedentary existence, presumably agricultural, but they were pushed west into a hostile coastal and island environment by the advance of the Ópata and the Pima at some time before the arrival of the Spaniards, perhaps as the end stage of a chain of reactions that was set off when the Apache groups began to move south. Agriculture was impossible in the new environment, which extended from the northern Cape Tepoca to the Guaymas Peninsula and included Tiburón Island,[14] and their diet assumed a strong marine orientation. Although McGee has probably exaggerated their reliance on marine animal food, it is true that the importance of vegetable nourishment declined.[15] Effectively, the Seri gradually lost contact with the tribes of the northwest cactus area and their culture degenerated. It is possible that the manufacture and use of alcoholic liquors may have been one of the cultural attributes that they once knew and lost. Mescal pits have been found on Tiburón Island, and the collection of pitahaya fruit along the Sonora coast was an important seasonal activity of the Seri. But apparently even the preparation of pitahaya syrup was unknown—probably through constant fear of the Pima and a desire not to be tied down to one spot on the mainland even for twenty-four hours.

The Guasave present an instructive contrast with the Seri. They, too, were nonagricultural, in a similar environment, with a survival of pottery. They, however, used fermented liquors to such an extent that an early observer could write:

> They are much given to wine, for they have many fruits of which it is made. During the three months when they are in season drunkenness is almost continuous, and dancing so frequent and long continued that it seems that those who engage in it must have superhuman forces.[16]

The difference may be partially explained in that the Guasave spoke a Cáhita tongue, and thus were in a position to maintain effective cultural contacts with the agricultural Cáhita to the northeast, whereas the Seri represented an island of Yuman speech surrounded by hostile Uto-Aztecans. We may assume that the use of alcoholic drinks, unless known and proscribed by prohibitions, represents additional knowledge and hence a higher cultural state than their nonuse. It is of course possible that the Seri never did have fermented liquors, that their fission from the Yuma-speaking tribes to the north by the intrusion of the Pápago antedates the diffusion of the alcohol complex into Yuman culture, and that they reached their cultural cul-de-sac already at a more primitive level.[17]

The natives of Baja California were too remote from Central Mexico ever to have come in contact with the alcohol complex. Of course they had no pottery or watertight baskets, but the local turtle shells would probably have served just as well. There was a great deal of fermentable material,[18] including pitahayas, tunas, and mescal, not to mention the sweet manioc of the south, and the "honey-dew" droppings of insects.[19]

The relation of peyote to alcohol is discussed in more detail in chapter 5 on the tuna and mesquite region. Suffice it to say here that its early use in the non-alcoholic region of the north is most obscure, mainly because of the late influx of Apache groups with their northern cultural affiliations. There seems to be no way of telling, for example, whether the pre-Lipan sotol people of the Big Bend region used peyote. The Apache themselves took to the drug very slowly. As late as the second half of the eighteenth century the Lipan had no intoxicants of any sort.[20] The earliest record in the literature of peyote consumption north of the Rio Grande appears to be for 1709, and refers to the Caddo of eastern Texas.[21] In 1719, peyote intoxication was recorded in Taos Pueblo.[22] As peyote grew neither in the lands of the Caddo nor in those of the Pueblo Indians, it is likely that an earlier learning process created a demand for peyote far beyond its natural range and made it an article of trade. After a long period of dormancy, Indian peyotism revived under a quasi-Christian guise, and in the late nineteenth and early twentieth centuries swept the Plains of the United States, reaching even into southern Canada and into the basin-range country of the west. The movement is still progressing with some vigor.[23]

Another aboriginal beverage in the non-alcoholic area is the well-known "black drink" of our southern Indians.[24] The drink is made from the dried leaves and tender shoots of a holly, *Ilex cassine*, that is native along the Atlantic and Gulf Coasts from Virginia to the Colorado River of Texas.[25] The beverage is reminiscent of the *yerba maté* infusion of Paraguay and Brazil, made from a related species, *Ilex paraguayensis*. The main physiologically active component of both drinks appears to be caffeine.[26] In addition, the drink from holly shoots contains a rather large proportion of tannin. On boiling, it acquires a characteristic black color. The intoxicating effect ascribed to the beverage as used ritually by the natives was due not to alcoholic fermentation, as has been claimed, but rather to the addition of certain alkaloid-containing drugs.[27]

TWO

Mescal and Sotol

Among the most important and widely used food plants in the seasonally dry regions of Mexico and Central America belong a certain group of the genus *Agave* that are collectively known as "mescal." Before the development of agriculture, mescal probably occupied the most widespread role in the native diet of Mexico northwest of Tehuántepec. No pottery is needed in its preparation. Mescal for food, and possibly for drink, was so widespread a complex that it cannot be treated adequately in terms of the other drink areas. It was the universal understory upon which the later food resources were superimposed, and it was apparently basic to all regions except the tropical lowlands.[1] Where agriculture came in[2] the original importance of mescal became somewhat obscured, or led to secondary developments, as in the case of the great pulque agave of the southern part of the central plateau. But if mescal became less important as a food supply, giving way to agricultural crops like *huauhtli* (*Amaranthus paniculatus*) and to the great triumvirate of maize, beans, and squash, it was still available as an emergency resource in times of scarcity.[3] (See Map 2.)

We may assume that people were early on attracted to the thick, quick-growing, juicy flower stalks of *Agave*, *Yucca*, and *Dasylirion*. In the dry areas of the north, the stalks were often cut off and sucked for their juice.[4] It would have been a logical procedure to roast the flower stalk, as was already done with many roots, to see if it could be eaten. When it was found to be sweet and nutritious, it apparently quickly became a staple food. The Tamaulipec used this process,[5] and it is likewise mentioned as an occasional practice among the Navaho.[6] Very likely Fages saw yucca stalks baked in the same way in California (as is discussed in note 22, below). The *relación geográfica* of 1777 for Jesús María y José states that the Cora bake and eat the flower shoots of four kinds of *Agave* ("*magueyes, mescales, masparillos,* and *tepemet*") and one kind of *Yucca* ("*isote*").[7] Lumholtz mentions a similar utilization among the Tarahumar of an amole (soap root) maguey.[8]

Map 2. The mescal wine region.

The next logical step in areas of thick-budded agaves would have been to bake the whole fleshy part of the plant after chopping off the tough, fibrous leaves, thereby making a much greater food supply immediately available and adding the further advantage of freedom from seasonal scarcity.[9] Thus, we come to the typical pattern of mescal utilization and the roasting oven, which in its various forms extends to southern Oaxaca.

Taxonomy and Nomenclature

The genus *Agave* is exceedingly diversified. For this group of the *Amaryllidaceae*, whose center of distribution lies in north-central Mexico, Trelease lists 170 species for Mexico alone, while Berger gives 274 in all, both authors admitting that their enumeration is incomplete.[10] All members of the genus are native to the New World, and range as far north as Utah and and as far east as Maryland, and at least as far south as the upper Magdalena basin in

Figure 2. A barranca landscape in Jalisco. The rugged canyon is in the Huichol Sierra, with fallow cornfields on cleared open slopes.

Colombia. The wild agaves of Peru are most likely escaped colonial introductions.[11] The species of the West Indies show a great diversity of form, somewhat differentiated from those of the mainland,[12] and are probably to be thought of as having undergone a distinct evolution since the disappearance of the (Pliocene?) land bridge to Yucatán and Honduras. (Figure 2.)

That the genus as a whole is native to arid climates is shown by the moisture storage adjustments in the typical fleshy leaves and bulky crowns or root stalks, and by the tough, scarcely permeable epidermis. The highland steppe country of central Mexico (*BS*) is the most typical environment, followed immediately by the somewhat moister highland rim with summer rainfall (*Cw*). Of the true deserts (*BW*), the genus is rather less characteristic, although desert species are fairly plentiful in Sonora and adjacent regions. Similarly, the hot lands with summer rain (*Aw*) show a marked reduction in species, while the lands with no dry season, whether they be hot (*Af*) or temperate (*Cf*), are generally quite lacking in indigenous agaves.

Since the various members of the genus are not easily differentiated in terms of form or function, except in rather large groups of similar utility, only a few proper names are widely current. The most common name today is "maguey," a word native to the Antilles, of Ciboney or Taino origin, and introduced by the Spaniards into Mexico. The word properly refers to all members of the genus, but is most commonly used in the Mesa Central for the great pulque agaves, and seems never to have been much employed in the northwest. The Nahuatl word for agave in general was "*metl*,"[13] to which various prefixes were added to differentiate species or closely related groups of species. Similar words (*mec, met, meke*, etc.) are found in many of the Uto-Aztecan languages. In the Northwest, where the pulque agave or maguey does not occur, the word "mescal" (also spelled variously "mezcal" and "mexcal") is used, derived evidently from *metl* and *ixcalli*, the latter meaning "cooked" or "baked."[14] Consequently, the term "mescal" should be restricted to those forms that were baked and used for food aboriginally.

Another name—widely current, although of exceeding vagueness—is the Spanish word "*lechuguilla*," literally, "small lettuce," which was originally applied by the conquerors to most small forms of agave having a symmetrical leaf pattern. Generally, they have a smaller central core than the mescal, and are not so convenient for roasting. This distinction is by no means rigid, however, and the word means very different things in different places. Thus, in the towns of Zapotlán, Sayula, and Apango, Jalisco, the word is actually applied to a variety of pulque agave, and in a number of other places (e.g., Autlán, Jalisco, and Bacanora, Sonora), it is used for a variety of mescal.

Zapupe and henequen are large, slender agaves that have assumed considerable commercial importance as sources of fiber. The former is found along the eastern escarpment of the Mesa Central, the latter in Yucatán. They were probably not used as sources of food aboriginally in the same sense as mescal since they do not show the necessary thickening of crown or leaf base. However, the Tamaulipeca's baked flower shoot may well have come from a zapupe form.[15] Waste from the henequen was used in the early twentieth century in the commercial manufacture of alcohol.[16] A similar utilization is not documented aboriginally for the Maya. Aboriginal mescal wine was invariably predicated on the manufacture of baked mescal for food. (See Figure 3.)

MESCAL FOR FOOD

The northern limit of mescal baking starts in the west with the Diegueño, but excludes their close relative, the Kamia of Imperial Valley,[17] for the reason that mescal is practically absent from the valley bottom. From the Cahuilla of the Peninsular Range to the tip of Baja California, mescal baking was of exceeding importance, the plants being found mainly in foothill locations at intermediate elevations.[18] Among the Yuma, the Maricopa, and the Mohave, mescal was scarce or entirely absent, while among the Cócopa of the lower Colorado, it seems to have been of great importance. Farther to the north, the limit swings west to include the Chemehuevi and the Southern Paiute. The

Figure 3. A *peyotero*, recently returned from pilgrimage to San Luis Potosí. Note cultivated *Agave* sp., or "*maï*" in background. At Rancho de la Mesa, Nayarit, December 1938.

northern Yuman tribes of Arizona, the Walapai, Havasupai, and Yavapai, found mescal to be an outstanding source of food supply. Of the Pueblo people, only the Zuñi baked mescal in former times; the plant is not found in their present territory.[19] When the Apaches descended on the mescal country, they soon learned to roast the plant; and among the southern groups, it became the most important single item of food. The Mescalero Apache derive their name from it. Toward the east, sotol (*Dasylirion* sp.), because of its greater abundance, to some extent took the place of mescal for food, especially among the Lipan and Toboso. The northeastern limit of pit baking follows fairly closely the valley of the Pecos–Rio Grande.[20]

Figure 4. An earthen pit utilized for baking or cooking agave stems. Near Rancheria San Andrés, Nayarit.

Along the seaward slope of the Sierra Madre Oriental, south of the Huaxteca Veracruzana, the abundant rains did not provide an environmental advantage to forms of agave with thick buds or turgid leaves. The resultant slender forms were essentially inedible, except for the *quiote* or flower stalk, and there was little necessity to seek it out in this land of tropical plenty and advanced hoe culture.[21]

North of the boundary just defined (see Map 2), agave was not baked, mainly because mescal forms did not occur,[22] while to the south the trait reached almost without interruption as far as the Isthmus of Tehuántepec (see Table 1), and perhaps beyond.

To bake mescal was a simple process. In a pit of variable size—usually roughly circular, from three to ten feet across and from one to four feet deep—a fire was made of brush or wood, and stones the size of cobbles were thrown in (see Figure 4). When the fire died down, the hot stones were positioned into a single layer and mescal heads were piled on top into a domelike heap whose thickness depended on the depth and diameter of the pit. A compact layer of fresh grass or moistened hay (*zacate*) was usually placed over the mescal, and the whole mound was tightly sealed with a layer of earth. After one to three days of roasting, the time depending on the size of the pit and the amount of mescal being processed, the mound was torn down and the mescal removed. The material

Figure 5. A mound of baked agave stems, *cabezas de mezcal*, prior to extraction of the sweet juice for fermentation.

now had a rich brown, somewhat translucent appearance, was sticky to the touch and sweet to the taste—an excellent and nutritious food. Usually the tender cores of the mescal heads were eaten immediately on removal from the oven because they did not keep well, while the more fibrous exterior to which the fleshy leaf bases were still attached was commonly pounded into a flat layer and dried in the sun, after which it would keep for a long time. This dried material could be used at any time by soaking it in water for an hour or so. Sometimes it was boiled into a kind of soup, although more commonly it was merely softened in cold water, and the soluble nutriment was sucked out from the mass of inedible fibers. Another widespread method was to soak the dry cakes in water until softened and to drink the sweet, turbid liquor that remained after the fibers were removed. In many regions this liquor was allowed to stand for a few days before being consumed, and thus it fermented into an agreeable wine.[23] (See Figures 5, 6, and 7.)

The essential thing that happens in the baking process is the hydrolysis and breaking down of complex carbohydrates into simple sugars. Neither glucose nor starch is found in the original material, but there is a large proportion of a mucilaginous gum that is hydrolyzed by the catalytic action of a small amount of free organic acid that is present.[24] A liter of the expressed juice of baked mescal, if left to dry, yields 450 grams of solid material, almost all of which is glucose.[25]

Figure 6. A commercial mescal factory with a large, stone pressing wheel powered by mule team.

Figure 7. The same mescal factory showing the pressing pit with the fibrous agave remains.

I can attest from personal experience that baked mescal is toothsome as well as nutritious. Such was also the verdict of the first Spaniards who tried it, for Motolinía writes: "many Spaniards like it as well as good *diacitron* (lemon peel preserved in sugar)."[26]

Mescal Wine

An examination of Map 2 and Table 1 shows that mescal wine did not extend as far north as the baking of mescal for food, although an unfermented drink from baked mescal is recorded for at least five tribes along the northwestern boundary. Among the Zuñi there is a tradition that mescal wine was made in former times, presumably when the tribe was living in an area farther to the southeast, where mescal grows. Although the use of mescal wines was very widespread at the time of the Conquest, it seems nowhere to have been the most important alcoholic drink, except perhaps among the Cora and the Tepehuán. (Figures 8 and 9.) Generally speaking, all the tribes that used it had at least one other beverage that was more important to them. Yet, at an earlier time, it is likely that mescal wine outranked other alcoholic beverages. The whole pulque complex may be an outgrowth of a mescal utilization, as suggested in chapter 7. In the *tesgüino* area, Lumholtz records that the Tarahumar considered the agave they called "*tshawi*" (recorded by Bennett and Zingg as *tcaweke*) as "the first plant God created."[27] The liquor made from it is considered indispensable for certain ceremonies.

It is probably safe to assume that wherever a mescal distilling industry arose in the colonial period, an undistilled mescal drink was known in pre-Columbian times, which in turn was predicated on the roasting of a plentiful resource of wild mescal plants for food. The introduction of the process of distillation was so early, the product of the stills so attractive to the natives, and the stills, once seen, so easily fashioned from native materials, that mescal wine soon came to be looked upon almost everywhere as merely an intermediate stage. Only among the remote and conservative groups who kept pretty much aloof from the Spaniards, and who were likewise beyond the influence of the galleon ports of the Pacific, was the undistilled product able to maintain itself. The one area in which it has survived to the present is the Tarahumar country, a forbidding land, difficult of access, peopled by some of the least changed Indians in Mexico.

Bennett and Zingg, after discussing the use of two kinds of mescal for food among these people,[28] describe the preparation of the wine as follows:

Both varieties of *Agave* are commonly used for *tesgüino* in the lowlands where *Agave* is plentiful and corn is very scarce. It makes a sweeter and more palatable drink than a *tesgüino* made from corn, as I [Zingg] had occasion to observe. The

Figure 8. The upper portion of a Cora still. The external receiver is made from an agave leaf.

Figure 9. In Nayarit, a Cora still on its hewn rock base. Note lower chamber where firewood is inserted.

hearts are cooked, as for eating, and then pounded in a hollow rock with the oak maul, as the highlanders pound their cornstalks. After they are well pounded, three or four large ollas of water are mixed with the pulp by treading on it with none-too-clean feet.

A framework of sticks is built across the hollow in the rock, and the maguey pulp piled on it to drain the liquid back. Then the pulp is twisted in the typical fiber net, *mabihimala*, just as cornstalks are, in the preparation of *tesgüino* [see Figure 10].

The root *gotóko* (*Leguminosae*) is pounded and put in the liquid, possibly as a ferment, although my information says that the juice is sweet and does not need a "ferment" of wild oats. Now the liquid is ready to strain through the basket-sieve into large ollas. It is boiled for two or three hours. When cool, the liquor will ferment in four or five days, although the addition of sprouted corn, fermented in the "boiling pot," will hasten the process to two or three days.

Often this maguey preparation is mixed with corn and prepared as for corn *tesgüino*. The bark of *Randia echinocarpa* is sometimes added as a ferment. Either pure or mixed it is called *batáli*.[29]

Immediately adjacent to the Tarahumar on the west lives a closely related tribe, the Varohío. The people make mescal wine also, and call it by essentially the same name, "*batari*."[30] To the fermenting mixture is added the root of a vine, *mawo* (W.), (*Phaseolus caracalla*).[31]

SOTOL

Particulars about aboriginal sotol utilization are surprisingly scanty. The great age of sotol pit baking in the Big Bend country has been established without question. From there the region of sotol utilization seems to follow the border lands between the *tesgüino* region and the tuna and mesquite region as far as the Huichol. The word "sotol" is derived from the Nahuatl, or, at least, from a Uto-Aztecan language. The Nahuatl equivalent given by Siméon is *çotolin*, which he translates as *palmier*.[32] In the area indicated, the term "sotol" refers invariably to one of the numerous species of *Dasylirion*,[33] and it is in this sense that the word is used here (Figure 11).

To a certain extent, sotol seems to be marginal to mescal. It fulfills the same functions for food and drink, and is exploited aboriginally by the same processes, but appears all in all less desirable and able to replace mescal only where the latter is scarce or of poor quality or where the sotol shows unusually attractive forms. Thus, while species of *Dasylirion* occur from New Mexico to Oaxaca, they were rarely utilized for food and drink outside the restricted area indicated above. The aboriginal economic importance of sotol has been obscured by the marginal character of the utilization, by the colonial introduction of stills, and by the lack of

Figure 10. *Pozos*, or fermentation pits, five to fifteen feet above the mean river level, that were hand hewn into the yellowish gray sandstone bedrock. In the vicinity of Guadalupe Ocotan, Nayarit, 1938.

Figure 11. Henry Bruman holding a sotol plant (*Dasylirion* sp.), 1938. (Photo by Bodil Christiansen)

Figure 12. A *canoa*, or hollowed log, of *huizilacate* wood (*Bumelia laetevirens*), with men holding *pizones*, elongated pounding tools to mash the baked sotol.

botanic thoroughness in the early observations. It is probable that the term "*lechuguilla*" was sometimes applied to sotol forms just as the term "sotol" has occasionally been applied to agave.[34] (See Figure 12.)

It is not known whether sotol is used anywhere for human food today.[35] Bennett and Zingg make a curious statement about its utilization by the Tarahumar. Referring to *Dasylirion durangense*, they say:

> After the trunk of this plant is roasted in the pit it is discarded. The Indians do not use it either for food or to make a distilled drink. . . . It is rather surprising that the Tarahumaras do not use the trunk for food, and it is possible that they do and that we did not happen to see them.[36]

I would like to know why the sotol trunks were roasted in the first place. The Huichol apparently use sotol only to make a distilled drink. It is in the manufacture of sotol brandy that they employ the famous primitive still that

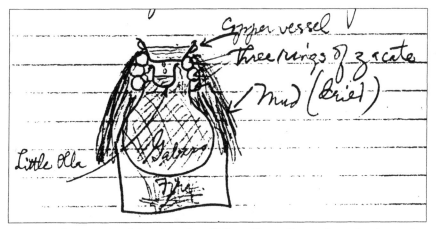

Figure 13. Cross-sectional drawing of a still from Henry Bruman's notebooks, 1938.

Lumholtz thought was indigenous, but that appears actually to be of Asiatic design. (See Figure 13.) By a reasoning process similar to that used with mescal, I would postulate that among the Huichol, sotol was aboriginally baked for food and fermented to make a simple wine.

In various parts of Durango, sotol (*D. durangense*) is fermented and distilled commercially today. The industry undoubtedly has an aboriginal base to it. Hrdlička also describes the use of sotol brandy among the Tepecano of Azqueltan in the valley of Bolaños, Jalisco.[37]

It is not to be supposed that all forms of sotol have a similar appearance. *D. durangense* consists of a clump of daggerlike leaves a yard long, attached to and entirely surrounding a cabbage-sized "head," which weighs between four and ten kilos. The sotol of Texas is like this compact form, but also belongs to species that have trunks up to three feet high. The sotol of the Huichol is never of the cabbage-head variety, but grows to a height of over three feet, with the trunk alone growing to a height of thirty inches occasionally and having a diameter of six to eight inches. I did not see a mature sotol of this last form, but was assured by several people around a Huichol distillery at Guadalupe Ocotán, Nayarit, that those were the dimensions. *Dasylirion* has not been described from Nayarit or Jalisco, according to Standley and M. Martínez, but the plants there may represent the southernmost extension of *D. simplex*, which is found in Durango.

The trunk or head of the sotol contains over 20 percent carbohydrates, not counting cellulose, of which 4 percent is already in the form of sugar.[38] Much of the remainder is converted into fermentable material in the process of baking.[39]

Table i. Use of Mescal for Food and Drink

Group	Mescal Baked	Varieties Identified	Non-Alcoholic Drink	Alcoholic Drink	Authority, pp.
Non-Alcohol Region					
Diegueño	Yes	*A. deserti*		No	Gifford, *Kamia*, 23
Kamia	No				
Cochimi	Yes	*A. shawii* / *A. goldmaniana* / *A. deserti*		No	Sauer and Meigs, *Lower California* I, 292
Guaicuru	Yes	*A. margaritae* / *A. connochaetodon*		No / No	Bravo, "*Razon*" / Baegert, *Nachrichten*, 121, 123
Seri	No	No			
Cocopa	Yes	*A. deserti*		No(?)	Kniffen, *Lower California* III, 54
Yuma	No			No	Forde, *Ethnography*, 117
Mohave	No			No	Castetter, Bell, Grove, 42
Cahuilla	Yes			No(?)	Spier, *Havasupai*, 119
Yavapai	Yes	*A. couesii* / *A. palmeri* / *A. deserti* / *A. parryi*	Yes	No	Castetter, Bell, Grove, 38–42
Havasupai	Yes	*A. utahensis*	Yes	No	Castetter, Bell, Grove, 38–42
Walapai	Yes	*A. utahensis*	Yes	No	Kroeber, *Walapai*, 49
Chemehuevi	Yes	*A. utahensis*		No	Kroeber, *Handbook*, 597
Southern Paiute	Yes	*A. utahensis*	Yes	No	Castetter, Bell, Grove, 45–47

Tribe	Use	Species			Reference
Hopi	No			No	Castetter, Bell, Grove, 54
Zuñi	Formerly / Yes			Formerly	Cushing, *Zuñi Breadstuff*, 635
Navaho	Yes (mainly quiote)			No	Spier, *Havasupai*, 119
Jicarilla	Yes			Yes(?)	Spier, *Havasupai*, 119 / Castetter, Bell, Grove, 60
Lipan	Yes (also sotol)	*A. lechuguilla* *A.* sp.		No	Sayles, *Arch. survey*, 62 / Bibl. Nac. Méx., "Costumbres," leg. 99, no. 66
		Dasylirion sp.			
Toboso	Yes			No	
Mescalero	Yes	*A. neomexicana*		Yes(?)	Castetter, Bell, Grove, 60
San Carlos	Yes	*A. parryi* *A. palmeri*		No	Castetter, Bell, Grove, 60
Chiricahua	Yes	*A. neomexicana*		Yes(?)	Castetter, Bell, Grove, 60
Coyotero	Yes	*A. couesii*	[Syrup?]	No(?)	Castetter, Bell, Grove, 60
White Mountain Apache	Yes (Mainly quiote)		Yes	Yes(?)	Castetter, Bell, Grove, 61–62
Jova	?			?	
Suma-Jumano	Yes			?	Pérez de Luxán, *Expedition*, 60
Concho	Yes			?	Pérez de Luxán, *Expedition*, 60
Coahuiltec	Yes			No	León, "Testimony," 37
Tamaulipec	(Only quiote)			No	Santa Maria, *Relación histórica*, 406
Pison Janambre	?			?	

Group	Mescal Baked	Varieties Identified	Non-Alcoholic Drink	Alcoholic Drink	Authority, pp.
Northwest Cactus Region					
Pápago	Yes	A. schottii A. palmeri A. deserti A. americana		Yes	Casetter, Bell, Grove, 47–48
Pima	Yes		[Syrup]	Yes	[Nentvig], *Rudo ensayo*, 82 Russell, *Pima Indians*, 70
Maricopa	Yes (rare)	2 kinds	Yes	No	Spier, *Yuman Tribes*, 55
Ópata	Yes			Yes	[Nentvig], *Rudo ensayo*, 50–51
Cáhita	Yes		Yes	Yes	García Icazbalcéta, 2d anon., in *Col. Doc. Hist. México*, vol. 2; 3d anon., in *Col. Doc. Hist. México*, vol. 2 *Mem. hist. Sinaloa*, 6 Perez de Ribas, *Historia*, 6
Tesgüino Region					
Tarahumar	Yes (also sotol)	A. patonii A. schottii "Lechuguilla" Dasylirion durangense		Yes	Lumholtz, *Unknown Mexico* Bennett and Zingg, 148–49, 163–67
Varohío	Yes			Yes	Gentry, *Warihio*, 1963

Group				Reference
Tepehuan	Yes		Yes	Perez de Ribas, *Historia*, 574
Huichol	Yes (also sotol)		Yes	Lumholtz, *Unknown Mexico*, vol. 2, 38, 186
Tecual	No(?)		?	No mescal mentioned in *relación* of Yscatun, Nayarit, July 29, 1777
Cazcan	Yes		?	*Noticias varias*, *Relación* for Tequaltiche, 1584, 349
Tuma-Mesquite Region				
Guachichil	Yes		Yes	Casas, *Libro*, 161
Pame	Yes		Yes	
Chichimeca Jonaz	Yes			
Zacatec	Yes		Yes	Arlegui, *Chronica*, 158
Lagunero	Yes	2 kinds	No(?)	Mota y Escobar, *Descripción Geográphica*, 56
Pulque Region				
Huaxtec	Yes		Yes	Tapia Zenteno, *Noticia*
Otomí	Yes		Yes	Paso y Troncoso, *Relación* for Texcatepec, 1579, in *Papeles*, 2d series, vol. 6, 33
Mazahua	?			
Tarasco	No(?)			Not in *Relación de Mechoacan* nor in *Relaciones geográficas*

Group	Mescal Baked	Varieties Identified	Non-Alcoholic Drink	Alcoholic Drink	Authority, pp.
Nahua	Yes				Paso y Troncoso, *Relación* for Chilapa, 1582, in *Papeles*, 2d series,vol. 4, 36; *Relación* for Tepeaca, 1580, in *Papeles*, 2d series, vol. 5, 180
Zapotec	Yes				Paso y Troncoso, *Relación* for Miaguatlán, in *Papeles*, 2d series, vol. 4, 129
Mixtec					Paso y Troncoso, *Relación* for Guaxilotitlán, 1581, in *Papeles*, 2d series, vol. 4, 199
Mixe	?				
Mescal-Jocote Region					
Tahue	Yes			Yes	Garciá Icazbalcéta, 3d anon., in *Col. Doc. hist. Méx.*, vol. 2, 451
Acaxee	Yes(?)				
Xixime	Yes(?)				
Totorame	Yes(?)				
Cora	Yes			Yes	Arias y Saavedra, *Informe*, 1673, *in* Santoscoy, "*Nayarit*," *Col. doc. inéd.*, 13
West Coast, lowland Nahua	Yes			Yes	Relación for Ystlahuacan, 1778, *in* Paso y Troncoso, Papeles, transcript in Museo Nacional de México

THREE

The Northwest Cactus Region

THE SAHUARO AREA

Of the great columnar cacti, the sahuaro (*Carnegiea gigantea*) is of special interest, for the fermentation of its fruit in the preparation of an alcoholic drink represents the northernmost extension of the traditional ritualistic use of alcoholic beverages in pre-Columbian America. Here and there farther northward, sporadic use of fermented drinks may have occurred, as suggested before, but with the sahuaro wine of the Papago, Pima, and Maricopa begins that great and continuous area of ritualistic drinking that extends southeast without interruption to beyond the Tropic of Capricorn.

The natural distribution of the sahuaro extends from the Yaqui River to the southern part of the Colorado Plateau (see Map 3).[1]

To the east and north its occurrence is limited by the minimum temperature of the coldest winters at an altitude of about twelve hundred meters. Westward the area reaches to the Colorado River and extends beyond in only three places, where the boundary appears to be determined as much by the fact that the rain falls only in the cold months as by the fact that the deserts of California, in which the cacti seldom occur, are usually dry. The plant is much more abundant in the northern than in the southern part of its ranges.

The species reaches its greatest display on rocky, eroded slopes with coarse, stony soil, being only scantily distributed on soils of finer composition, and lacking entirely of the heavy diluvial type. Over its entire range it is widely distributed on mountain slopes facing southward. The region of its optimum development lies between five hundred and one thousand meters, and above fifteen hundred meters only a few specimens are to be found. It does occur in Sonora, Mexico, at sea level, but whenever found below two hundred meters in altitude rarely attains the size and strength necessary for forming branches.[2]

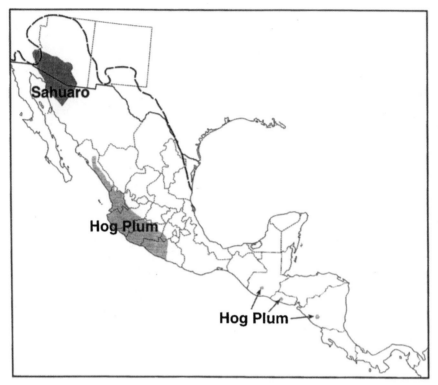

Map 3. The sahuaro and hog plum regions.

Forrest Shreve has found that

> the plant seldom attains a height greater than twelve meters, and that it reaches a maximum age of 150 to 175 years. Flower formation begins when the plant is three to four meters high and fifty to seventy-five years of age. The flowers appear in May and become densely formed under the apial growing region on both the main stem and the branches. The fleshy fruits ripen five to six weeks later.[3]

The fruit of the sahuaro was used for food originally by the Papago, Pima, Maricopa, Yuma, Yavapai, Walapai, Western Apache, and Seri, whereas the manufacture of sahuaro wine was carried on only by the Papago, Pima, and Maricopa.[4] The harvest season lasted from the middle of June to the middle of July, and generally represented the high point of the year for the Indians in or near the sahuaro region. A number of tribes carried on lengthy migrations to the best sahuaro plots at that time. So important was the sahuaro season in the native economy, and such a complete change from the rest of the year, that two of the tribes, the Papago and the Pima,[5] started their yearly reckoning with the sahuaro harvest. It was the only time of the year when there was more food available than could be readily consumed. The people ate and grew fat and made merry, especially the wine makers, and much of what they could not consume they prepared for future use.

By means of a long cactus pole or crook, the fruit was knocked down from the top of the plant. The pulp, scooped out with the thumbs, was thrown into baskets, later to be transferred to clay pots. After a process of boiling, straining, and boiling down, there remained a brownish syrup and a mass of fiber and seeds.[6] The syrup, when mixed with from one to four times[7] its volume of water and allowed to stand in earthen jars, readily fermented into an intoxicating beverage. The established time for fermentation was two or three days.[8] During fermentation, care was taken that the must did not become chilled. For this purpose a fire was usually kept going in the neighborhood of the fermenting jars, and the Papago sometimes put blankets over the jars.[9] The blankets were "to make it strong without so much of the bad taste," which evidently means that the Papago had discovered empirically that the particular microorganism engaged in the fermentation was most efficacious at uniform, fairly high, temperatures. Usually a small jar of fermented liquid was used for seeding large jars that were slow in starting to ferment,[10] and if many jars were fermented at the same time for the sahuaro festival, the contents were usually poured back and forth so that the fermentation was completed simultaneously in all of them.[11]

The resulting wine, called "*navai't*" by the Papago, was a crimson colored liquid "with a slightly nauseating taste, which, when drunk in the ritual quantity, induced vomiting. It was almost impossible to keep this beverage, therefore the tradition was that the whole supply must be consumed within twenty-four hours."[12] Apparently no analysis of the beverage has ever been made, but judging from the process of manufacture and from the great quantities imbibed by the participants in the sahuaro festival, it is unlikely that the alcohol content exceeded 5 percent. Neither is anything known of its composition or nutritive value.

The Pitahaya and Tuna Area

In southern Sonora and northern Sinaloa, beverages from the pitahaya (mainly *Lemaireocereus thurberi*) and from the tuna (*Opuntia* sp.) took the place of sahuaro wine, although there was some overlapping among the southern Papago. The various genera of pitahaya have a much wider range than the sahuaro,[13] being found through most of Baja California, parts of southern

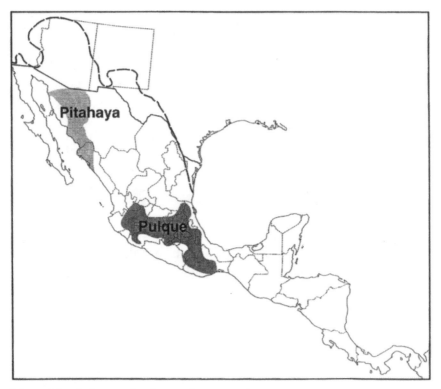

Map 4. The pitahaya and pulque regions.

Arizona, throughout the hot, seasonally dry valleys of the western and eastern Sierra Madre of Mexico, the drier parts of southern Mexico, Central America, and northern South America, and even in the West Indies, where the name "pitahaya" was first encountered by the Spaniards.[14] The use of the pitahaya fruit for food is evidently very widespread, but its use for an alcoholic drink is recorded only from this northwestern area, where *Lemaireocereus thurberi* is the main species (see Map 4).

This organ-pipe cactus seems to be even more particular in its temperature requirements than is sahuaro, and in southern Arizona is rarely found except on the warmer slopes of the lower and more southerly mountains. Hence it does not appear in such large numbers nor in "forests" as does sahuaro. It is, nevertheless, rather abundant in parts of Sonora and the Indians prefer its fruit to that of *Carnegiea*. According to Shreve, the occurrence of this plant in Sonora is confined to rocky slopes and coarse outwash and is more common on south slopes than on north ones.[15]

This plant is even taller and more massive than the sahuaro, and its fruit has a better flavor, although the syrup made from the fruit is said to be inferior to sahuaro syrup.[16] The seasonal rhythm of utilization is not nearly so marked as in the case of the sahuaro, for *L. thurberi* usually bears fruit twice a year, from May to August, and again in October.[17] The manufacture of the alcoholic beverage was in general similar to that of sahuaro wine, and need not be further described. *Lemaireocereus* has not been reported from Sinaloa,[18] and the "pita-haya" used there aboriginally as a source of an alcoholic drink may have been a different plant.

The name "tuna" for the prickly pear was likewise introduced from the Antilles by the Spaniards, and refers to the fruit of the nopal cactus.[19] Its Aztec equivalent is "*nochtli*." The main center of varietal diversity of the nopal seems to occur on the Mesa Central around San Luis Potosí and Zacatecas. There, the nomadic hunting and gathering tribes made use of the fruit as one of their chief sources of food and also as a source of a fermented drink, as discussed in chapter 5. In the area around the Gulf of California, the nopal was of relatively lesser importance because this area is far richer in edible plants than is the central part of the plateau. The important thing about the nopal as a source of food and drink in northwestern Mexico may have been that its many varieties[20] insured a longer seasonal supply of sweet fruit than could be obtained from the pitahayas. Pfefferkorn, however, contradicts this hypothesis, stating that tunas were ripe in Sonora only during one month ("in June").[21] He records the existence of two main varieties, one white, one pale red. There was a third variety that was sweeter, and the cochineal tuna was different still. He remarks also that the tuna was not so common as the pitahaya in Sonora and that its flavor was inferior.

The use of tunas in the manufacture of an intoxicating drink in this area is recorded for the Pima, the Ópata, and the Cáhita, including the Guasave. Nowhere in the literature of these tribes is the process of making the drink described in detail, which is probably an indication that it was not generally of outstanding importance. Perhaps the procedure was similar to that used with the sahuaro and pitahaya, namely a preliminary boiling down to a syrup followed by dilution and fermentation, although this was not the method used in the tuna and mesquite region. A wine from the fruit of a cholla cactus (*Opuntia cholla*) was observed among the Ópata by Hrdlička.[22] It has not been reported elsewhere, but may have been included by the older chroniclers under the term "tuna."

In addition to the cactus drinks already mentioned, a fermented drink from baked agave heads was everywhere characteristic except in the far northwest among the Maricopa. The Papago also had a kind of weak *tesgüino*, made as follows: "they grind fine some dry corn, mix it with water, and then strain the mixture and let it stand until it is partially fermented. The liquor tastes bitter and is too weak to make them drunk."[23] Its weakness and bitterness was evidently due to lack of malting and the presence of unfavorable bacteria. The complete process of brewing *tesgüino* was found in this area only among the Pima,[24] the Ópata,[25] and the Cáhita[26] (excluding the Guasave), and is described in detail in chapter 4. For the Pima, a wine from elderberries (*saúco*) is reported that was so potent that intoxication lasted for three or four days.[27] This severe intoxication cannot be ascribed to ethyl alcohol; it must have been caused by either higher alcohols or esters, due to a peculiar fermentation, or by alkaloids. A similar drink has already been mentioned for the Indians around the San Gabriel Mission in southern California. Hrdlička mentions a wine from wild grapes for the Ópata, basing his statement on the following citation from the *Rudo Ensayo*: "The Indians eat a wild grape . . . but . . . the quality [of a sample], to my thinking, is very caustic. I have seen them make vinegar and also brandy from it."[28] On the basis of this statement alone, it is not valid to assume that the Ópata made a wine from wild grapes aboriginally. Pfefferkorn also mentions wild grapes, but says nothing regarding their aboriginal utilization. He states that a brandy was sometimes made from them, but that the few stills in Sonora were exclusively in the hands of the Spaniards.[29] To my knowledge an aboriginal wine from wild grapes was not made by any natives in the New World.

An alcoholic drink from mesquite pods was evidently prepared in certain parts of the northwest cactus region. This concoction is mentioned for the Cócopa,[30] the Pima, Papago, and Ópata,[31] and possibly for the Cáhita.[32] The final beverage cited in the literature for the area is mead, made by fermenting diluted honey, and is described by Perez de Ribas for the Cáhita as the "most highly esteemed and best tasting" wine they had.[33] The honey was gathered in the mountains from the nests of wild, stingless bees, not much larger than ordinary flies.

The most characteristic technique in the northwest cactus area for preparing alcoholic drinks was to dilute and allow to ferment a syrup that had been made by boiling down the juice of ripe cactus fruit after first straining off the pulp and the seeds.

FOUR

Tesgüino

Centered in the Sierra Madre Occidental is an area in which a beer from sprouted maize is the most characteristic intoxicating beverage. This beer, generally called "*tesgüino*" in Mexico, occurs in a region that aboriginally overlaps north into the area of giant cactus drinks and south into the fringes of the pulque region. In parts of Central America and cordilleran South America, a similar beverage is made, although in many cases the conversion of starch into sugar preparatory to fermenting is accomplished not by malting (sprouting), but by chewing. The latter drink is generally called "chicha," and its ethnological relationships are discussed in more detail in chapter 9.

The heart of the *tesgüino* area appears to extend from the Tarahumar to the Huichol and Cazcan, with a lesser emphasis among the Tepehuán. In this area the use of *tesgüino* is inextricably intertwined with the roots of economic and ritualistic life. A strong secondary center is found among the Mazahua of the Valley Toluca, although the picture there is somewhat obscured by the occurrence of pulque. Between these two centers, reference to *tesgüino* occurs sporadically. "*Vino de maiz*" is casually mentioned, for example, in the *relación geográfica* for Chilchota, Michoacán, of October 15, 1579.[1] Beaumont emphasizes strongly, although apparently without justification, the former importance of maize beer in the ritual life of the Tarascans.[2] Farther to the north, the beverage has survived somewhat better. The town of Arandas is even today well known for its *tesgüino*, and *tesgüino* vendors come all the way to Guadalajara to make and sell their wares. It is barely possible, however, that the spread of *tesgüino* into this area may have been post-Conquest, for the Jiménez Moreno map makes the Arandas area aboriginally Guachichil. An early occurrence of the drink for the Cazcan region proper is well authenticated. The report of the *visita* to Nueva Galicia of the *oidor* Daualos y Toledo in 1616 mentions *vino de maiz* and *pulque de maiz* for Mestiticacan (Mexticacan) and Suchipila (Juchipila).[3] Both terms

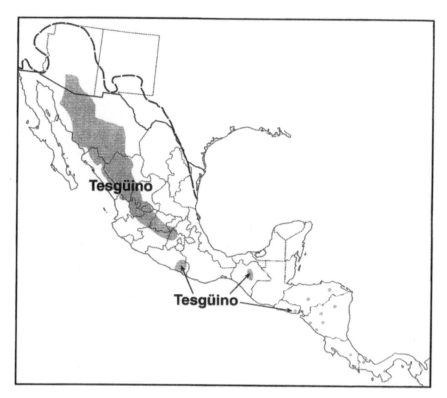

Map 5. The *tesgüino* regions.

undoubtedly refer to *tesgüino*. Throughout the whole area from the Cazcan country to the Valley of Toluca, one is left with the impression that pulque had come in from the east shortly before the Conquest and that it was gradually replacing the earlier *tesgüino*. In fact, pulque pushed even farther to the west, taking a foothold in the mountain lands of the Cora, where *tesgüino* was apparently unknown.[4] (See Map 5.)

Among the Huichol and the Tarahumar, the importance of *tesgüino* in a native society reaches its zenith. In the culture of both groups, its use is a ritual necessity at practically all festivals and, among the Tarahumar, it has a powerful economic function as well. Its apparent unimportance among the intervening Tepehuán is puzzling. Sixteenth-century documentation regarding this issue has not been found. Perez de Ribas mentions only wine from mescal and "other wild fruits" for the Tepehuán.[5] A mid–seventeenth-century report of the Mission of San Pablo, which was part Tarahumar and part Tepehuán, records that the common native drink was made from maize and was like the beer of Flanders.[6] From this, we can of course draw no inferences as to pre-Columbian Tepehuán culture. Preuss lists *tesgüino* for the Tepehuán; Lumholtz, only for the northern Tepehuán.[7] A letter by Estteuan Lorenzo, Bishop of Durango, to the viceroy, dated December 10, 1790, goes into great detail about drunkenness among the Tepehuán, but refers almost exclusively to distilled mescal and does not mention *tesgüino* at all.[8] It is evident, then, that *tesgüino* was not important among the Tepehuán in colonial times. A reconstruction of aboriginal culture is made difficult by the fact that thoroughgoing Spanish contact antedated the first description of the Tepehuán by many years.[9] The introduction of stills via early Spanish mining endeavors may have shifted the emphasis from maize to mescal. For some reason corn whisky was shunned.

Tesgüino played an important role also among the agricultural tribes to the west and north of the Tarahumar. Lumholtz observed its use among the Tubar,[10] and for the Ópata, Cáhita (excluding the Guasave), and Pima it has already been referred to in chapter 3. The Jesuit carta anua of 1593 relates: "They make also wine from the same maize, and at times have solemn drink festivals [*borracheras*], for which the whole town congregates, although they do not allow youths [*mozos y gente nueva*] to drink."[11]

One of the four ritual dances of the Yaqui that survived into the nineteenth century was called "*tesguín*."[12] The impression remains, however, that for the Cáhita *tesgüino* was merely one of several important ritual beverages, with mescal wine and various cactus wines also having a significant place. The same observation applies to the Ópata and the Pima. In the far north, the manufacture of *tesgüino* takes on certain aberrations due to the peripheral location. It is possible that there were two advances of the practice of *tesgüino* brewing northward along the Sierra Madre Occidental: once, when it was imperfectly learned by the Papago and the Zuñi, and then again, much later, when the trait was transferred to the Apache.

NOMENCLATURE

The term "*tesgüino*" appears to be derived from a Uto-Aztecan language, most probably Cazcan, which is closely akin to Nahuatl. We have no adequate study of the Cazcan dialect, but by virtue of close analogy the etymology of the word can be explained on the basis of Nahuatl. Rémi Siméon lists "*teyuinti*. What intoxicates someone, to get intoxicated," which is related to "*iuinti*. To be drunk, to take to drink."[13] "*Te*" is an indefinite relative personal pronoun. It would appear, then, that the word is really *te-i-uin-o* and that there is no relation whatever to the Spanish word for wine. The final *o* may be a post-Conquest suffix due to Spanish influence, as it is not essential to the word and is not always used. Many variant spellings are found in the literature (e.g., *tejuino*, *tesvino*, *texuino*, *tizwin*), but "*tesgüino*" seems to be the most common and approaches most closely to the usual sound of the word when Spanish orthography is followed. The *s* or *z* sound may have come into the word in colonial times. The Huichol, when pronouncing the word, come very close to "*teuino*" even today, as do also the natives around Guadalajara.

It is significant to note that although the word has a very general derivation, it is applied specifically to one beverage. This is one of the main reasons for supposing that corn beer had a long history in the Cazcan area and that it had no serious competitors in the pre-pulque epoch.

In languages less related to Nahuatl, we find other terms. The native Huichol word is "*nawá*," although a Huichol of Ratontita told me that *me-yéN* (nasal) is another name for it. The malted corn ready for grinding is called "*dátzú*." For the Tarahumar, we have the native name "*xuhuiqui*,"[14] which Bennett and Zingg also found and wrote as "*suwíki*." The borrowed term "*tesgüino*" seems to be used by the Tarahumar also in reference to mescal wine, and to the product of joint fermentation of maize and baked mescal.[15]

The name "*sendechó*" is applied today to corn beer in the region of the Mazahua and the neighboring Otomí, especially around Ixtlahuaca, north of Toluca. It is evidently a hispanicized form, derived according to Mendoza and Orozco y Berra from the Ótomí word "*zeydethâ*," which is composed of *zey*, meaning "pulque" (i.e., fermented drink), and *detha*, meaning "maize."[16] Soustelle agrees with the indicated etymology, but his transcription may be more precise.[17]

THE BEVERAGE

If there is any preference in the *tesgüino* region regarding the type of maize to be used for brewing, it seems to have gone unobserved and unrecorded. It would be indeed strange if there were not. When I was in the field I was unfortunately not concerned with this possibility. At Guadalupe Ocotán, Nayarit, a consultant stated that "*mais amarillo*" would make the strongest *tesgüino*. This may have been flint corn. In the preparation of chicha in the cordilleran area of South America, there seems to be a decided preference for flint corn, if we may believe Velasco.[18]

The first step in making *tesgüino* is to malt the corn. The procedure consists of moistening the grains, shielding them from the light, and allowing them to produce colorless sprouts to a length of an inch or so. While the sprouts are forming, and as a result of the action of enzymes called "diastases," which occur naturally in an inactive state in cereal grains and become activated on sprouting, a large proportion of the starch present in the kernels is converted into fermentable sugars. This process, known as saccharification, can take place only through the chemical addition of water and, from the functional point of view, consists of the conversion of insoluble stored-up carbohydrates into soluble forms, thus allowing them to be transported to the growing parts of the plant where they are needed.

After the malt is ready, it is ground, boiled for many hours, diluted—often with the addition of other ingredients—and then fermented. The process as explained to me by a *tesgüino* vendor from Arandas is as follows.

Maize kernels are put on a petate (reed mat) or *costal* (sack) in a thin layer, and are covered by another petate or *costal*, so that no light strikes them. Water is sprinkled on top intermittently, and the kernels produce white sprouts about an inch long in five or six days. If the kernels were not covered, the sprouts would be green and bitter and would give a bitter flavor to the *tesgüino*. The white sprouts are sweet. The kernels and sprouts are well ground on a metate, and the mass is put in an olla with water to boil. For good *tesgüino*, the boiling continues for twenty-four hours, with continuous stirring and with the addition of fresh water whenever needed. After twenty-four hours, the boiling mixture is a fairly homogeneous syrup. Water is carefully added to the syrup and the diluted sweet liquid is put in an olla in the shade to ferment. It is ready to drink in twenty-four hours. (See Figure 14.)

The process just described is the traditional one. The consultant also described a modern procedure, according to which the maize is not put to sprout, but is merely soaked in water for about six hours. Panocha (brown sugar) is then put in, in addition to water, and the liquid is allowed to ferment. The post-Conquest vulgarization of the process is obvious.

For the Tarahumar we have the detailed description of Bennett and Zingg:[19]

Three to five decaliters (*amúl* from Sp. *almud*) of corn are shelled into a basket or sack, thoroughly moistened and kept in an olla for two or three days in a warm place. Then a hole 12–18 inches deep is dug where the sun strikes the ground. It is lined with pine needles or grass. The wet corn is put in this hole and covered with pine needles and a layer of small stones. The corn is kept moist in this hole until it sprouts. When the sprouting has advanced to a satisfactory stage, the corn is taken out and ground on the metate two or three times. Then, with plenty of water, it is placed in a large olla and boiled all day until it becomes yellow. White beer is not acceptable.

It is now ready to take off the fire and be cooled. When it is cool, the liquid is strained through a special basket, *warí* (basket) *págera* (from *pagé*, "to strain"). It comes out looking like *esquiate*, and has a not unpleasant sweet taste. It is at this

Figure 14. A Huichol woman prepares traditional tortillas at fiesta. The clay olla beside the tortillas holds corn beer, or *tesgüino* (*nawá*). Rancho de la Mesa, Nayarit.

stage that the process is complicated. From his [*sic*] cornhouse the Indians take about a pint of brome grass, which resembles oats, *basiáowi* (*Bromus* sp.), and which has been gathered and saved for this purpose. This furnishes the ferment and is an essential ingredient of *tesgüino*. It is ground on the metate, but is not cooked, as it would not ferment.[20]

Wild oats are sometimes ground with a quantity of lichen (*Usnea* sp.), which they think stimulates fermentation and makes the liquor sweeter. Other methods of sweetening the liquor include the four moss-like plants magora (*Selaginella cuspidata*), and which are often ground up in the drink, too. Other plants are added to change the flavor: *dowísawa* (*Chimaphila maculata*), to make it stronger, and the root of the *dolinawa* (*Stevia* sp.), which also makes it stronger, especially when the *tesgüino* goes flat. It sweetens it as well.

We drank *tesgüino* wherever we went, and it showed a great difference in taste. This was partly due, no doubt, to the various mixtures of plants. Several bunches of the sedge (*Fimbristylis* sp.) are often ground with the corn to prevent colds.[21]

The combination of ingredients for fermentation are put in a special small olla (*síkokí donéla*, "boiling-pot"), which has "learned to boil well," i.e., to ferment. These special pots are carefully kept for this use alone and are never washed or used for cooking, as their facilities might be impaired. The Indians say that these pots learn how to "boil" from each other. The "boiling-pot," thus filled, is placed in a warm place near the fire, where it ferments all night. The next morning its contents are mixed with the strained corn liquid, and it ferments within three or four days. It is then ready to drink.

Distilled drinks are not made by the Indians, although *sotol* is bought from the Mexicans. I was told that in some places the Tarahumaras get the effect of distillation by sealing up the *tesgüino* pots in fermentation with lime and allowing the process to go on for a long time.[22]

According to Lumholtz, Huichol *tesgüino* is thicker and much sweeter than that of the Tarahumar, "to which it is inferior in every way. It is also used more sparingly than in the north, but, as there, exclusively for religious purposes."[23] The corn is sprouted on a low sandpile, covered with grass and sticks and watered regularly. After six days, when the sprouts have formed, the corn is ground, and boiled for thirty-six hours with water, which must be replenished often. The mass is then diluted and strained into gourds. In twelve hours, the *tesgüino* is ready to drink, in spite of the fact that no ferments of any kind are added.

The method of the Mazahua in preparing their *sendechó* is essentially similar to the preceding, except that the fermentation is seeded from a previous batch and different auxiliary herbs are used.[24] The traditional sprouting procedure calls for a basket lined and covered with the leaves of the *tepozán* tree (*Buddleia* sp., probably either *B. americana* or *B. sessiliflora*), which is filled with the moistened maize and placed in the sun for four or five days. The leaves of the *tepozán* have a fine camphoraceous odor that is imparted to the moistened kernels, but it is unlikely that the aroma survives the process of boiling and fermenting.[25] Their use may have had some obscure ritualistic significance. The flavor that was added with a conscious desire to modify the taste of the final brew was that of red chile, which was ground with the malted maize.[26] A bland variety was used, from which the more caustic veins and seeds had been removed. The seeding mixture was called "*ixquini*," and its addition allowed the fermentation to proceed to completion in two days.[27] On top of the fermenting mixture a thin, red-colored, oily layer appeared, which was carefully separated and added in small quantities to each draught of the brew consumed.

As in other parts of the *tesgüino* region, symbols of degeneration of indigenous culture traits have appeared in the Mazahua country. A *sendechó* vendor in Ixtlahuaca told me that the process of boiling the malt is no longer done. The sprouted maize is merely ground and fermented in water for about a day. The result is a cream-colored, unstable liquid that has a tendency to form a thick sediment. It usually contains less alcohol than free, unfermented sugar.[28] The use of chile for flavoring is rare nowadays, and there is a tendency to fortify the poor

Figure 15. Temple group of Huichol *peyoteros* recently returned from the long walk to Real de Catorce, in San Luis Potosi State. Rancheria de la Mesa, near Guadalupe Ocotán, Nayarit, December 1938.

result of imperfect brewing by the addition of pulque or aguardiente, or even to change its character entirely through the use of brown sugar or orange juice.

If we may judge by taste and intoxicating power, an average *tesgüino* made by the traditional process would be about as strong alcoholically as ordinary barley beer, or perhaps a little stronger. An estimate of 4 or 5 percent alcohol would not be far from wrong, although an analysis of an unadulterated sample seems never to have been made. The beverage in this sense is nowadays brewed only in remote sections of the sierra, and it is hard to keep and hard to transport. A sample tasted at the Huichol rancheria La Mesa near Guadalupe Ocotán, Nayarit, at a peyote festival on December 13, 1938, was perhaps somewhat inferior to the usual run. It was a dark, murky liquid with the appearance of milky coffee, and tasted like a weak, sourish beer with an unmistakable flavor of corn. An objectionable amount of gritty sediment was included in the sample, probably from ashes that had blown in during the boiling and fermenting. But for its weak alcoholic taste and thinner consistency it was rather reminiscent of an off-color, half-soured atole. (See Figure 15.)

Figure 16. Gourds used in extracting aguamiel from maguey plants in Actopan, Hidalgo, Mexico, 1938.

Competing Drinks in the *Tesgüino* Region

In addition to the dominant *tesgüino*, there were several other beverages of some importance in the area. Mescal wine and cornstalk wine had a wide distribution, and sotol wine may have been used by the Huichol and the Tepehuán, as already indicated. In the south, pulque was actively encroaching on the *tesgüino* area at the time of the Conquest, and the late-sixteenth-century Tlaxcalan colonies caused it to spread even more. For the purpose of mapping, all areas in which pulque and *tesgüino* occurred simultaneously have been put into the pulque region, since pulque became the dominant beverage almost immediately.

Lumholtz records a brandy made from *guayabas* (*Psidium guajava* L.) for the Huichol.[29] (Figure 16.) Whether it was known aboriginally in undistilled form is impossible to say. It must be a nauseating beverage to the uninitiated, since the big yellow *guayabas* have a peculiar odor that is repugnant to most people on first acquaintance. According to Lumholtz's consultant the drink tastes good, but leaves a headache. Nowhere else has an aboriginal drink based on the *guayaba* been observed. The Navarro report of 1784 mentions a *"pulque de guayaba,"*[30] but this is merely a mixture of mashed *guayabas*, sugar, and ordinary *pulque blanco*, and is no doubt a concoction of the *refresco* type of drink having a colonial origin.

In part of the northern Cazcan area, *colonche* had apparently encroached from the east. This cactus wine is said to have been used by the Xiconaqui and Custique tribes living on the plains of Tepechititlán.[31]

FIVE

Tuna and Mesquite

The central part of the Mexican plateau west of the *tesgüino* region and north of the great pulque area was sparsely settled in pre-Columbian days by a number of tribes—in the main, migratory and nonagricultural—who, in the first year of the Conquest, were lumped together under the general term "Chichimeca." They occupied a great interior area mostly of steppe climate (*BS*), with occasional enclaves of desert (*BW*) in the south and an extensive longitudinally elongated desert core in the north, while the mountainous southwestern rim was temperate winter dry (*Cw*). In general, they were the people north and northwest of the Otomí. With the establishment of mines in the heart of their region in the mid-sixteenth century, they were found to speak various languages and they were subdivided into Zacateca, Guachichil, Pame, and a residuary group of Chichimeca (Jonaz). Later exploration and settlement in the north added the Pison Janambre, Tamaulipeca, Coahuilteca, Lagunero,[1] and Toboso to this general group of simple hunters and gatherers. Their range covered an immense area, from southern Guanajuato and Querétaro to the Rio Grande, and from western Durango to the Gulf of Mexico. (See Maps 6 and 7.)

Among the most characteristic vegetation forms are members of the genera *Agave* (mescal), *Dasylirion* (sotol), *Yucca* (isote), *Prosopis* (mesquite), and *Opuntia* (nopal) as well as other Cactaceae. All these were edible and fermentable, although there were many local differences in their utilization. Thus, alcoholic drinks were not recorded for the Pison Janambre, Tamaulipeca, Coahuilteca, and Toboso, although their available plants were not greatly different from those of other tribes. True, the tunas became inferior toward the north,[2] and the agaves grew less fleshy toward the east coast, but there was still a great abundance of fermentable material, especially mesquite.

Pedro de Aumada, in his detailed report of March 20, 1562, concerning the rebellion of the Zacateca and Guachichil Indians mentions mesquite and tuna as

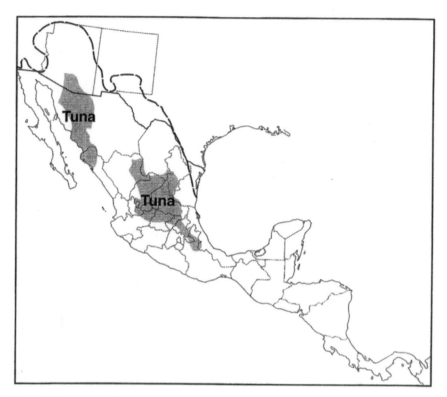

Map 6. The tuna regions.

the main food of these tribes. The mesquite harvest lasted three or four months, and when it was over the natives moved on to the *tunales*, where they remained for eight months. He relates that they had a great quantity of white tunas and various kinds of red ones, one of which was like the sort common around Mexico City (*Opuntia ficus-indica*?). Others were eaten with their rind (*O. leucotricha*?) and were the most common and "the most gentle and healthful food." He recounts also the tale of a black who was caught by some Indians not far from Zacatecas and threatened with death during a drunken feast.[3]

A few years later, Gonzales de las Casas wrote a lengthy account that includes all of the southern Chichimeca groups.[4] After stating that they bake mescal as well as various kinds of roots, he remarks:

They have their beverages which they drink, for up to now no tribe has been found which is content to drink only water. The Mexicans have only the one they

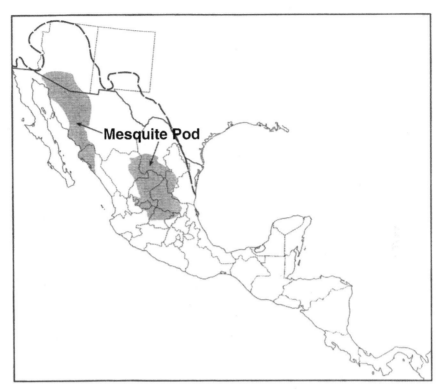

Map 7. The mesquite pod regions.

draw out of maguey. These have the same,[5] and others which they make of tunas, and still another of mesquite, so that they have three different kinds of wine with which they get drunk very often, for they are drunkards in the highest degree. They have no vessels of pottery or wood, but only a sort which they make of fiber so closely woven that it will hold water. In these they make the wine, and some of them are as big as a canasta [large basket]. Because of their experience with the dangers of drunken brawls it is their custom when drinking that the women go off by themselves and hide the bows and arrows. According to what I have learned they never all get drunk at the same time, but always leave some to keep guard, so that they should not be surprised when drunk and taken unawares or killed.

The item regarding the fermentation of drinks in watertight baskets is of considerable interest, for it refutes those culture historians[6] who have claimed that a knowledge of pottery making is prerequisite to the use of fermented drinks. Arlegui adds the information that large supplies of wine were sometimes made when neighboring groups convened in a joint council of war, and that these supplies were kept in hollowed-out barrel cacti (*biznagas*).[7] Some of these could hold as much as six *arrobas* (about twenty-five gallons). Over great stretches of the Chichimec country, running water is absent during most of the year, and potable springs are rare. Cardenas relates that some of the Chichimeca were accustomed to do without water entirely, eating tunas instead, and sucking the juices from green nopal branches and from the flower stalk of the lechuguilla.[8] The story is certainly true at least in part, and it is easy to see how a fermented beverage from the fruit juice of cacti would furnish a refreshing accent in a pretty monotonous diet. Here and immediately to the south in the Otomí region, where aguamiel and pulque fulfilled a similar function, the drinking of alcoholic liquors was probably less inclined toward ritualism and more toward filling ordinary dietary wants than in any other part of Mexico.

Of the many different kinds of wild tunas found in the tuna and mesquite region, the most highly prized is the cardona, from the *nopal cardón* (*Opuntia streptacantha*). It is an almost globular purplish red berry, up to two inches in diameter, and comes from a treelike platyopuntia that grows as high as sixteen feet. This cactus is one of the most common native plants of the old Chichimec area, and it may possibly have been the most important single source of food for aboriginal inhabitants. There were in addition at least a dozen other platyopuntiae that were economically important, not all of which have been completely classified. The data are summarized in Table 2.[9]

A few varieties of columnar cacti with edible fruits occur in the area, among which *Lemaireocereus queretaroensis* ("pitahaya") and *Myrtillocactus geometrizans* ("garambullo") are the most important. The *Cylindropuntiae*, however, generally have inedible fruits, and were probably not utilized very often. Any or all of the edible species listed above may have been used in the preparation of alcoholic drinks in pre-Columbian times—there seems to be no specific information on aboriginal preferences—although it seems likely that the cardona tuna, by virtue of wide and plentiful distribution and excellent characteristics, was then as now the most important food and drink cactus in the region.[10]

Tuna wine is called "*colonche*" today in the San Luis Potosí area. The name is evidently a scrambled form of its early counterpart, "*nochocle*" (the form found in official literature until the late eighteenth century), which in turn is a slightly modified version of the Aztec "*nochoctli*," from *nochtli*, tuna, and *octli*, wine.

The process used in its manufacture by the hunting and gathering tribes in this region is described by Alegre, who says, referring to the Chichimeca around San Luis de la Paz:

Every third day the women make the wine, and the men drink so much that they lose their senses. The material from which this liquor is made is the tuna. The way to make it is to remove the rind, strain the juice through sieves of straw, and put it by the fire or in the sun, where it will ferment vigorously inside of an hour. As this sort of wine is not very strong, their intoxication lasts only a short time, and they soon come back for more.[11]

Alegre's description is particularly interesting because it shows clearly that no boiling down of the fruit juice was involved. Indeed, these tribes had no impervious vessels that could resist direct contact with fire. They seem not to have been acquainted with the process of stone boiling. Even if they had known the process, it would not have helped in this case; it is impossible to boil down a sugary liquid with a hot stone without ruinous caramelization and general decomposition.

In the *relación geográfica* of Coscatlan (Coxcatlán), dated July 11, 1777, we find the following:

There is another [plant] which they call Cardona. . . . The Indians exploit it and make a drink of it called Nozhotle [*sic*] which is highly prized by them. But it must be consumed at exactly the right stage in the fermentation, for it is palatable neither before nor after. The greatest length of time during which this beverage will keep is scarcely twelve hours.[12]

That the cardona was important in the preparation of tuna wine is further brought out by the extensive report compiled by Juan Navarro, Director General of Alcabalas y Pulques during the administration of Gálvez.[13] The report, dated February 29, 1784, mentions six kinds of alcoholic drinks made from tunas. For two of these drinks, the cardona is specifically indicated, for a third, the *tapona*, while the rest merely call for tunas in general.

Nochoctli was a rather weak wine, as already mentioned in the quotation from Alegre (*Historia*). The same might be surmised from the analysis of sugar content given in Table 2. Fermentation experiments have been made with tunas, and it was found that the juice of *Opuntia laevis*, which appears to contain rather less sugar than the cardona, gave as much as 5 percent alcohol after fermentation with a good wine yeast.[14] It is probably safe to infer that the cardona will give a 4 to 5 percent wine even when fermented with wild organisms.[15]

The other characteristic drink of the region was made from mesquite pods, and in the southern part of the area, they seem to have been used mainly during the first four months of the year when ripe tunas were not available. The mesquite (*Prosopis chilensis*),[16] also written "mezquite" (from Nahuatl *mizquitl*),

TABLE 2. *Platyopuntias* of Economic Value in the Tuna and Mesquite Region

Common Name of Fruit	Classification	Plant	Fruit	% Total Sugar (as Dextrose) in Edible Portion*	Remarks
Tuna cardona	*Opuntia streptacantha*	Treelike, up to 16 ft. high.	Subglobular, up to 2" in diam. Deep red. Also a rarer light yellow form.	8.22 to 11.05	
Tuna pachona	*O. streptacantha* var. (?)	Treelike, 10 to 15 ft. high.	Red purple. Similar to cardona.	9.12 to 9.31	
Tuna chaveña Tuna caidilla Tuna cascarona	*O. hyptiacantha* var. (?)	Treelike, 10 to 12 ft. high.	Obovate red. Similar to cardona, but slightly longer and ligher in color.	9.12 to 9.39 (For chaveña; others not given.)	These three closely related.
Tuna tapona	*O. robusta*	Treelike, up to 16 ft. high.	Globule to ellipsoid, 2¼ to 3½" long. Deep blood red.	9.39	
Tuna cuija	*O. cantabrigiensis*	Round bush, 4 to 7 ft. high.	Globular, 1½" in diam. or slightly ellipsoid. Dark purple throughout.	4.18	
Tuna de castilla	*O. ficus-indica*	Large and bushy, or treelike, up to 16 ft. high.	Ellipsoid, 2 to 3½" long. Red or yellowish green.	?	

Tuna durasnilla	*O. leucotricha*	Treelike, 10 to 16 ft. high.	Variable, 1 to 2¼" long. Light yellow or mottled red. Aromatic.	7.08 to 8.84	Rind usually eaten with pulp.
Tuna joconostle	*O.* sp.	Treelike, 7 to 10 ft. high.	Subglobose, 1¼" in diam. or obovate. Deep red or yellowish green.	4.76 to 7.74	Several kinds, probably specifically distinct, but none edible until baked.
Tuna vinatera	*O.* sp.	Open, branching plant, 12 to 15 ft. high.	Ovoid, 1⅛ x 1⅞". Dull red.	10.22	Popular name and high sugar content suggest use for fermentation.
Tuna agua-mielilla	*O.* sp.	Treelike, 10 to 25(?) ft. high.	Subglobose to obovate, 1½" long. Deep red.	8.84	Much used today for *miel*, *melcocha*, and *queso de tuna*.
Tuna leonera	*O.* sp.	Treelike, 15 ft. high.	Almost globular. Deep dull red.	10.78	

* The column on sugar content is based on analyses by D. Griffiths and R. F. Hare, *Prickly Pear and Other Cacti as Food for Stock*, New Mexico Agricultural Experiment Station Bulletin no. 60 (Albuquerque, 1906).

will grow into a forty-foot tree where moisture conditions are favorable, but in dry regions it takes the form of an irregular shrub with a strongly developed, deeply penetrating root system. The slender pods are four to ten inches long, bear exceedingly hard black seeds (which are generally discarded), and have from 25 to 30 percent glucose in the matrix pulp.[17] After being pulverized in a mortar,[18] the meal from the pods could be baked into a kind of bread,[19] or mixed with water and drunk as a kind of gruel, or fermented with the addition of water into a wine. In the north, where the tunas became less desirable, the role of the mesquite became correspondingly greater in the native economy. Thus, mesquite wine is the only fermented drink recorded for the Lagunero, although other alcoholic drinks are not specifically excluded.[20] Unfortunately, we have no precise details as to the preparation of the beverage in this region, where it assumed such an important relative position. It would be interesting to know whether the wine was made by fermenting the clear liquid that was obtainable by decanting the supernatant liquor in a dilute mesquite gruel or whether the sediment was allowed to remain. Another missing item of considerable significance is what the proportion of pounded mesquite pod to water would be, since the strength of the final brew depended on it.

Sahagún, without specifying the place, tells of a drink made by fermenting the inner layer of the bark of the mesquite,[21] although this may be an error, since no one else has verified it. Such a procedure is not entirely improbable, however. It reminds one of Hrdlička's Apache beer, made from the inner bark of the pine,[22] and of certain "*mecate*" beers in Central America, discussed in chapter 9. The inner bark of the mesquite is sweet, and hence fermentable; the San Carlos Apache sometimes put it into their *tesgüino* for sweetening purposes (see Table 2).

The northern part of the tuna and mesquite region is the aboriginal center of the peyote cult,[23] and the widespread use of this plant may be partially ascribed to the relative unimportance of fermented drinks. Sahagún was undoubtedly right when he stated that those of the Chichimeca who used peyote did so in place of wine.[24] It must not be inferred, however, that the two were mutually exclusive in a rigid sense; they were more properly supplementary and, to the extent that strong drink was ritualistic, partially interchangeable.[25] (Figure 17)

The center of distribution of peyote lies in San Luis Potosí, Nuevo Leon, Coahuila, Chihuahua, Durango, and Zacatecas.[26] An outlier is found in southern Querétaro, and a large and almost continuous area, covering perhaps a hundred miles in width, extends along both sides of the Rio Grande from a few miles below El Paso to the great eastward bend eighty or ninety miles beyond Laredo. The Big Bend country, including half the land between the middle Rio Grande and the Pecos, is part of this northern peyote region.

Figure 17. Henry Bruman conversing with a Huichol consultant in front of a traditional Huichol god house, a mud and stone structure with grass-thatched roof, November 1938. (Photo by Bodil Christiansen)

Peyote as a culture trait probably spread from somewhere in the north-central tuna and mesquite area. The diffusion was facilitated partly by the extensive natural range of the plant on the northern Mexican plateau, partly by the wide range and mobility of the hunting and gathering tribes that first adopted it, and partly by the powerful effects of the drug itself and its inevitable mystical associations.

To the north and northwest, peyote extended farther than fermented beverages. Among the Tamaulipeca[27] and the Coahuilteca,[28] neither of whom had alcoholic drinks, the trait was apparently well established in pre-Columbian times. The same is true for some of the people of the *tesgüino* region, as has been mentioned. Peyote ritual was strongly developed among the Huichol, slightly less among the Tarahumar and the Cora, and considerably less among the Tepehuán.[29] Toward the south, peyote was unimportant, both Sahagún and Hernandez referring it specifically to the Chichimeca and Zacateca groups.[30] The southernmost extension may have been found among some of the Otomí, although it is possible that diffusion to the Otomí may be post-Conquest.

SIX

Cornstalk Wine

Sugarcane, entirely unknown in aboriginal America, was one of the first economic plants to be introduced by the Spaniards. However, a sweet cane in the broader sense was not only known but widely utilized prior to the Conquest. The Indians had learned that green cornstalks contained considerable sugar; and in many and widely separated areas, it was common practice to crush the stalks, collect the juice, and boil it down to a syrup. Crystallization of the sugar was not practiced because it always charred. The economic importance of cornstalk syrup was widely attested to by the early explorers and chroniclers. Cortés wrote to his king that it was on sale in the great marketplace of Tenochtitlán, as were honey and maguey syrup.[1] The *relación* of Mechoacán mentions "syrup from cornstalks" for the Tarasca.[2] As far south as Peru, cornstalk syrup was manufactured,[3] and as far north as the Iroquois, the sweetness of cornstalks was recognized.[4] Cornstalk segments were chewed for their flavor as sugarcane segments are chewed wherever sugarcane is grown. (See Map 8.)

Some tribes who made a syrup from cornstalks may have known the process of diluting it with water and letting it ferment. Most groups who made cornstalk wine, however, made the beverage directly from expressed juice without a preliminary concentration. The manufacture of syrup and the manufacture of wine may not have had more than a casual connection either geographically or technologically. At first glance, one might suppose that cornstalk juice would be directly fermented whenever obtainable and that diluted syrup might be substituted during off-seasons. This practice is nowhere recorded, however. Apparently other drinks, such as *tesgüino*, or pulque, or fruit wines of various sorts were considered superior and were made whenever possible. Cornstalk wine was mostly considered a low-class substitute beverage to be used when other sources of drinks were not in season, or, in the *tesgüino* region, to conserve the grain supply.

Map 8. The cornstalk wine regions.

The Tarahumar make a cornstalk wine even today, but boiling the syrup seems to be unknown. Their procedure in making the wine is given by Bennett and Zingg as follows:

> At harvest time, when there are plenty of fresh corn stalks, the stalks are used in place of the more valuable corn. Tesgüino made from stalks is called *patcili*. After the leaves are removed, the stalks are taken to a large hollow boulder and pounded with oak sledges. Then the juice is squeezed out of the stalks by means of a clever device, *mabihímala*, invented for this purpose. It is a net woven from *sóka* fiber (*Yucca* sp.) and is generally about 12 x 15 inches. This is woven to encircle a stick at either end. The sticks are about 18 inches long. One of them is held with the feet, while the other is held in the hands. All the juice that can possibly be twisted out of the pounded cornstalks is removed with the *mabihímala*. The juice collects in the depression in the rock, and the bagasse is thrown away.

The juice is mixed with water and is then ready to strain through the basket strainer (mentioned before). Afterward it is boiled for a couple of hours over the fire, together with the root of *gotóko* (specimen unidentified), which has been well ground. The *gotóko* root is a necessary ingredient in this preparation. The mixture is allowed to cool and left to ferment with about half a decaliter of sprouted corn to act as the ferment. Sometimes the fermentation of the cornstalk juices in the "boiling pot" serves as the only ferment. In about five days the liquor is ready to drink.[5]

According to Lumholtz the result is an "extremely distasteful" drink.[6]

For the Tepehuán and Huichol, we have no specific information about an aboriginal preparation of cornstalk wine. There is, however, one lead. In the 1784 report of Juan Navarro regarding alcoholic beverages in New Spain, *vino de caña* is mentioned for the town of Bolaños. *Vino de caña* as defined in the document is made by fermenting cornstalk juice by letting it ferment naturally and then adding a little brown sugar to sweeten it.[7] While the addition of the sugar was a colonial afterthought, the first part of the process was absolutely aboriginal and could not have been influenced by contact with the foreign mining population of Bolaños. The individuals using this beverage must have been natives, and, judging from the location, were either Huichol or southern Tepehuán (Tepecano).

In pre-Conquest and early colonial times, a similar beverage was made by the Mazahua, and possibly Otomí, in the valley of Toluca and Ixtlahuaca, although by now even the memory of it seems to have disappeared. The beverage was prohibited in 1608 under threat of severe penalties by Luis de Velasco, the second viceroy to bear that name.[8]

This edict did not succeed in eradicating the beverage, however, as the Navarro document still mentions *vino de caña* for Toluca, a century and three quarters after the law was passed. Other parts of the Central Plateau for which *vino de caña* is recorded are Guadalajara, Chautla, Tacuba, and Tezcoco. Under the name "*ostoche*," the beverage—this time entirely aboriginal without even the addition of sugar—is mentioned as far south as Teutitlán del Camino, Oaxaca. For Tehuacán, two beverages are described that are brewed from a mixture of cornstalk juice, pulque, and other ingredients. A very potent drink, called significantly the "bone breaker" ("*quebrantahuesos*") is listed for Tacuba and Texcoco. It is a concoction of cornstalk juice, toasted corn, and ripe seeds from the Peruvian pepper tree (*Schinus molle*).[9]

Likewise in the Totonac and northwestern Nahua area, the cornstalk drink seems to have been formerly of considerable importance. The *relación geográfica* for Xalapa de la Veracruz (Jalapa) of October 20, 1580, mentions that the Indians who speak "*mexicano*" have a native wine of sweet cane.[10] Nowadays this drink is no longer remembered in the thoroughly modernized neighborhood of Jalapa, but in some of the more remote sections to the northwest, a faint recollection of the beverage lingers on.

A field trip in the summer of 1939 that took me into the rugged hill country north of Zacapoaxtla, around Huitzila, Zongozotla, and Zapotitlán, brought some significant results. The most common intoxicating drink now used by the Mexicano population[11] around Zacapoaxtla and Cuetzalan is *xixiqui*, a drink distilled from the fermented juice of sugarcane. This is the beverage most commonly called "aguardiente" in other areas. During a conversation on the general subject of intoxicating beverages and distillation techniques, a consultant from Cuetzalan, without any specific prompting on my part, volunteered the information that, around 1905, he was told by an old Mexican, already past the century mark, that in his youth *xixiqui* was sometimes made from the fermented juice of cornstalks.

The highland Totonac around Zongozotla make an intoxicating drink today from a decoction of water, brown sugar, and *timbre* (or *timbrillo*).[12] For 25 liters of the beverage, a kilo of brown sugar and 25 *manojos*[13] of *timbre* are used. The beverage is drunk after fermenting about twenty-four hours. In certain remote places in the highlands, according to consultants in Zongozotla, it is made to this day from the juice of pressed cornstalks in the place of brown sugar and water. The Totonac name for the drink is *tazlcóm*, a term incorrectly translated by Patiño as "pulque."[14]

North of the Totonac area, for the town of Guayacocotla (now Huayacocotla), the Navarro report mentions a drink called "*zlizitle*," made by fermenting cane juice in a bark receptacle with certain herbs.[15] Finally, at the northernmost Gulf Coast outpost of aboriginal higher culture, among the Huaxtec, we find *vino de caña* mentioned again. Most interestingly, the Huaxtec word for cane wine, "*boc*," has its counterpart in other languages of the Maya family. A consultant from the Alta Verapaz of Guatemala described a modern Kekchi drink known as "*boj*" (Spanish orthography) that is made by fermenting sugarcane juice with toasted maize kernels. Translated into pre-Columbian equivalents, the recipe would call for cornstalk juice and toasted maize. This close correspondence in terminology among two groups as far removed from each other in time and space as the Huaxtec and the Kekchi would argue for the considerable antiquity of cornstalk wine.

SEVEN

Pulque

In the southern Mexican plateau, the utilization of agave for beverages has assumed a most distinctive form. In its barest outlines the process consists in waiting until the maguey is ready to sprout a flower shoot, "*quiote*," cutting out the heart of the plant, which leaves a large hole, and then removing and fermenting the juices that collect in the cavity. The method is unique, although it shows certain similarities to the African and tropical American processes of palm-cabbage tapping. An important difference is that palm cabbages can be tapped at any time, whereas the maguey can be tapped only when the *quiote* begins to emerge.

THE ORIGIN OF PULQUE

There are two ways in which the "discovery" of pulque can be explained on a rational basis. One would be to see the process as originating with the early utilization of the *quiote* as a foodstuff (described in chapter 2); the other, to regard it as a transfer of techniques from the tapping of palms in the tropics. At present, it seems impossible to decide between the two theories; both may have some truth to them. (See Map 9.)

The tapping procedure was used mainly on agaves that did not have a thick bud development. The pulque magueys fall into this class; most of their substance is contained in their heavily developed leaf bases. Accordingly, a prepulque mescal utilization in terms of *quiote* and leaf base is highly probable. Professor Maximino Martínez, the eminent Mexican botanist, informed me (personal communication) that even today individuals in the state of Hidalgo will delay baking the mescal for consumption until after the *quiote* is a meter long. Apparently, the state of Hidalgo is the most likely center of origin of the pulque complex. According to López de Gómara, eating the *quiote* and manufacturing pulque were not mutually exclusive activities, as is commonly supposed, but were combined in aboriginal

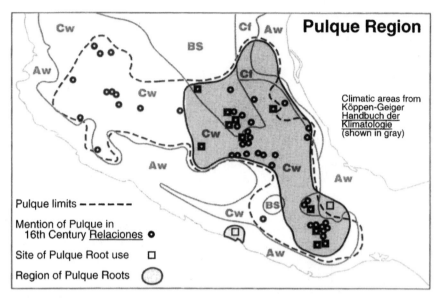

Map 9. The pulque region in detail. Climatic codes: Aw—tropical savanna, pronounced dry season; BS—steppe/grassland, less than 15" rain/yr; Cf—seasonal–midlatitude moist, midlatitude rainy, mild winter. Koppen, Geiger, *Hardbuch*.

utilization. The flower stalk was cut out when it was still short and tender, and was roasted and eaten. A hole was made in the bud from which the stalk was taken, and the liquid that collected there was made into wine and other products.[1] If, indeed, roasting of the *quiote* has the priority, it is easy to see how the second part of the process, the manufacture of pulque, may have come about. When a growing *quiote* is removed from a maguey, the open wound continues to exude sap for a considerable period. This sap is sweet to begin with, and it quickly ferments and spoils. Field rodents, birds, insects, etc. are greatly attracted to the sweet juice and may have called attention to its potential uses. Once it was found to be sweet and palatable, collecting it became a natural sequel in the process, especially when the additional potency that the juice acquired on aging a little was discovered. The most obvious method was to excavate a hole in the top of the bud into which the liquid could drain and from which it could easily be removed. At that moment, the long empirical evolution of the process of pulque making was under way.[2]

Agaves soon acquired an entirely new significance, and they were probably planted in fields with a conscious effort to select the best varieties. The utilization of the *quiote* for food must have declined greatly as soon as it was found that a greater yield of sap is obtained if the hole is cut when the shoot is just at the point of emerging.[3]

Rather surprisingly, the available evidence in mythology and religious symbolism regarding the original home of pulque points northeast in the general direction of the Huaxteca. The generic name of the Nahua drink gods was *Ometochtli*, "two rabbit," and according to the early records, there were four hundred gods in all, many of them with proper names of regional significance.[4] Seler has pointed out that many of the sculptures of *Ometochtli* show unmistakable Huaxtec influences in their dress, particularly in the frequent use of a conical cap of typical Huaxtec design.[5] The matter is particularly puzzling because only inferior pulque agaves grow in the largest part of the Huaxteca; they are specifically distinct from those of the plateau, and give a poor quality of pulque known as "*tlachique.*" Furthermore, there appears to be no particular designation for "pulque" in the Huaxtec language; "*tzim*" is both the recorded term for pulque and the general word for maguey.[6] Even today, only a small proportion of the native population of the Huaxteca has taken to pulque. The main Huaxtec drink today is aguardiente made from sugarcane,[7] and, as mentioned elsewhere, the common aboriginal intoxicants were cornstalk wine, tropical fruit wines, and, perhaps significantly, coyol palm wine.[8]

Sahagún also brings the Huaxtec (*Cuexteca*) into his story of the invention of pulque, but only in the role of early imbibers rather than as discoverers. According to him, the Olmeca, a group presumably related to the Toltec, were the first to make pulque:

> It was a woman who first learned how to tap magueyes for the honey from which the wine is made, and her name was *Mayauel,* and he who first found the roots which they put in the honey was called *Pantécatl.* And the authors of the art of *pulcre* making as it is done today called themselves *Tepuztecatl, Quatlapanqui, Tliloa, Papaztactzocaca,* all of whom invented the manner of making *pulcre* on the mountain called *Chichinauhia,* and because the said wine gives forth spume they also called the mountain *Popozonaltépetl,* which means frothy mountain.[9]

Immediately following this account is the story of the first pulque feast, at which everyone was given only four cups of pulque, not five, so that no one would get drunk. One Huaxtec chieftain had five cups, however, and in his drunken state took off his clothes, thus offending the others, who thereupon decided to punish him. The Huaxtec leader and his men subsequently fled back to their homeland, *Panotlan* (Pánuco), from whence they had come.

The legend shows not only that the auxiliary use of roots was a very early concomitant to aguamiel fermentation (see below), but also that the aboriginal home of pulque should probably be sought among the Nahua population somewhere immediately to the south of the Huaxtec. Seler has made a thorough study of the symbolism associated with ritual drunkenness among the Nahua, and he comes to the conclusion that the pulque gods, who are fundamentally harvest gods strongly linked to moon worship, may have had their origin near Metztitlán (Hidalgo), the "land of the moon"[10] (*metztli*, "moon"; *tlan*, "place of"). That this area was particularly consecrated to the pulque gods is further substantiated by aboriginal legends found in the vicinity of Metztitlán regarding Ometochtli which were sufficiently vivid to be recorded in some detail in the *relación geográfica* of 1579.[11]

The possibility remains that the Nahua may have derived the idea of tapping the agave from the Huaxtec palm-wine process, provided, of course, that the process was aboriginal. It is perhaps less likely that the Huaxtec would have extended the palm-tapping method to the agave, for we would then have expected a somewhat richer vocabulary. As mentioned, their word for pulque is the same as their general word for maguey. On this basis, it is possible that pulque is a recent acquisition for them. The precise role of the Huaxtec in the "invention" of pulque seems to be insoluble on the basis of existing information. That the Huaxteca must have been close to the center of greatest expansive power of the pulque complex is evidenced since it was the only region in which the drink extended into the tropical lowlands.[12] Although the Huaxteca Veracruzana lies toward the cool boundary of the *Aw* region of the central Gulf Coast, the temperatures are still much higher than on the plateau, and the average annual rainfall (circa 45 inches) is also too great to be favorable to the development of the large-sized pulque magueys.

At any rate, pulque seems to have originated not far from the northeast limit of the natural occurrence of the big, juicy magueys suitable for exploitation. From there, the complex spread extensively toward the west and the south. Throughout the colonial period and to the present day, the best pulque has come from the plain of Apam, not far south of Metztitlán. There, as the result of long-continued selection, the pulque maguey has reached its greatest development, and there is located the pre-Conquest settlement of Ometusco (originally, *Ometuchco*, the place of *Ometochtli*), dedicated to the pulque deity.

The Areal Extent of Pulque

The pulque agave was native to the "cold lands" of south-central Mexico, and its utilization in the pulque complex required a strictly sedentary population.[13] Since pulque was far superior to the earlier mescal wine, both in flavor and in amount of beverage available per plant, elaboration of the complex spread out nearly to its theoretical limits in all directions, starting from

Figure 18. Pulque pigskins in a courtyard in Pohuatlan, Puebla, 1938.

the hypothetical focus around Metztitlán and Apam. In the south, pre-Columbian pulque manufacture apparently stopped in the hill country to the west of the Isthmus of Tehuántepec; in the east, it advanced hardly at all because of the unfavorable climate along the escarpment of the plateau; and in the west, it pushed forward to the Pacific slope of Michoacán and Jalisco. Toward the north, its advance was slight because of a cultural rather than a climatic barrier. Here roamed nomadic wanderers for whom pulque manufacture was out of the question unless they became sedentary.[14] The limit there has been drawn somewhat to the north of the later site of Querétaro.[15] (Figure 18.)

The aboriginal limit is difficult to determine in the far northwest. The Cazcan group certainly fits into the *tesgüino* area, although pulque was probably known at least to the southern Cazcan. The *relación* of 1584 for Nuchistlan y Suchipila mentions that syrup, wine, and vinegar are made from magueys. That "syrup" is made would imply the "wine" is pulque and not mescal wine. But whether this utilization was pre-Conquest is impossible to decide without additional documentary information. At any rate, this neighborhood is not far from the aboriginal northwestern limit of pulque. The *relación* for Taltenango of 1584 mentions the use of magueys only for the curing of wounds and is silent regarding the beverage.[16] The plants were cultivated, however, and one must assume that this effort had behind it a more powerful urge than convenience in procuring medicines.

In the account of Mota y Escobar we find maguey syrup (from which we can infer pulque manufacture) listed for Suchipila and also for the town of Jalapa, some twenty miles to the north,[17] while Daualos y Toledo, some years later, gives pulque also for the town of Mestiticacan.[18] The last two items are not conclusive, however, since Cazcan economy was subjected to strong modifying influences before Mota and Daualos came upon the scene. In 1589, a strong colony of Tlaxcaltecas was established in Colotlan, not far to the north, and because the geomorphology of the region is such as to facilitate north-south communication, we must allow for the possibility that Tlaxcaltec pulque methods subsequently spread. These Nahuas intermarried with the Cazcans, and taught by precept their higher cultural techniques.[19]

Another intricate problem arises in the case of the Cora, who live about a hundred miles west of Colotlan. In terms of the heart of the pulque region, the Cora are the most remote tribe for whom the introduction of pulque is undocumented. The earliest account, that of Arias Saavedra from the 1650s, mentions that they had "*vino ó pulche*." While Arias speaks of mescal in a number of places, he nowhere mentions the pulque maguey, and it is more than likely that for him the word "*pulche*" means any sort of undistilled native beverage, a common usage in colonial Mexico.[20] Hence, he was probably referring to mescal wine. It is quite possible from the context that Arias did not intend to equate "*vino*" and "*pulche*," but that the former term was used for mescal brandy (distillation had probably come into the area by that time), which is still the practice in much of Mexico today. Ortega speaks of this *vino* a century later, and there is no doubt that it is distilled. Nor does Ortega mention pulque for the Cora, though he gives native words for maguey and for mescal brandy.[21] Yet, a few years later there is no doubt that the authentic pulque was being made by the Cora. The *relación* of 1777 for Jesús María José states: "There are also some pulque magueys under the general heading of '*Hiervas con q^e hacen vino*' (Herbs from which Wine Is Made)."[22] Sometime in the middle of the eighteenth century, the practice of pulque making, which is still carried on to some extent today, must have been introduced.[23] It may have come in either from the area south of Tepic or from Colotlan. Trade contacts were maintained by the Cora with both.

Toward the south, the aboriginal pulque limit probably reaches Autlán, where pulque is recorded in the *relación* of 1777,[24] and where it is still made to some extent today. Autlán (elevation about 3,000 feet) is the only place known to me where magueys of the kind that can be tapped for their sap occur side by side with coconut palms. Seaward from Autlán (e.g., in Purificación), pulque magueys are unknown. Still farther to the south, the boundary skirts the flanks of the Volcán de Colima, continues to Coalcoman,[25] and then veers abruptly eastward, passing to the north of the depression of the Rio Balsas to Ichcateopan,[26] and from there northeast to Tepoztlan.[27] The boundary then follows a general southeasterly direction, always avoiding the lowlands, until it comes to the Zapotec towns of Coatepec and Ocelotepec in southern Oaxaca. At this point the southernmost aboriginal extension of the pulque complex is reached. The line goes northeast from here, and reaches its easternmost limit in some of the high Chontal towns between Yautepec and Tehuántepec.[28]

The Pulque Magueys

The obvious physical differences between the pulque agaves of central Mexico and mescal agaves are greater size, much fleshier leaves, and a relatively slighter development of the central core or *cabeza*. On the plain of Apam, where the largest magueys of Mexico are cultivated, a specimen of *Agave atrovirens* approaching maturity may reach a height of more than ten feet and have a central diameter of fourteen or sixteen feet.[29] Yet, among pulque agaves there is a great diversity in form and sap yield. An early nineteenth-century work lists thirty-three different kinds for the plain of Apam alone, although the number of species is much smaller.[30] They range in size from inferior forms only three feet high that yield a low-grade sap over a period of only twenty days to the great "tractable, genuine maguey," with leaves growing as long as twelve feet, that yields excellent aguamiel for six months.

The problems of taxonomy and nomenclature in connection with the economic agaves of Mexico are highly intricate, and have not been completely worked out. Even the pulque magueys are satisfactorily identified only in part. The results of a recent study[31] that seeks to overcome the restricted point of view of most of the previous approaches to the problem are summarized regionally in Table 3.

W. Trelease gives half a dozen other species of maguey that are used today in the manufacture of pulque, including *A. weberi, A. complicata, A. gracilispina, A. melliflua, A. quiotifera,* and *A. crassispina.*[32] These, however, are all native to areas north of the aboriginal pulque region, and hence their earliest utilization for pulque must fall in the colonial period.

The edaphic requirements of the pulque magueys are not rigid. Being essentially plants of the high tropical steppe, they are at home on somewhat alkaline soils with a low humus content. On the Mexican plateau, the plants will reach maturity in from six to twelve years, the time depending on the variety and on local conditions of soil and climate. In very rocky areas in parts of the Mixteca

Table 3. Regional Summary of the Pulque Magueys

Species	Local Name	Area of Utilization for Pulque
A. atrovirens	maguey manso fino	Plains of Apam (parts of the states of Hidalgo, Mexico, and Tlaxcala)
A. atrovirens var. sigmatophylla	maguey de penca larga	Otumba, Mexico; Irolo, Hidalgo
A. lehmanni.	maguey corriente toloqueño, uña de gato	Plains of Apam, Valleys of Mexico and Toluca
A. salmiana* A. salmiana var. angustifolia*		Parts of the states of Puebla and Oaxaca
A. cochlearis*	maguey chalqueño	Southern part of Valley of Mexico
A. latissima	maguey de venado	Near Milpa Alta, D.F.**
A. mapisaga	maguey mapisaga	Near Tacubaya, D.F.

* Trelease considers *A. salmiana* and *A. cochlearis* as subforms of *A. atrovirens* (*in* Standley, *Trees and Shrubs*, 130). Berger (*Agaven*) makes them separate species.

** Also in Michoacán, according to Trelease (*in* Standley, *Trees and Shrubs*, 128).

Alta, full growth is not attained until the fifteenth year.[33] Seven or eight years is the usual period around Apam.

The Pulque Process

The procedures followed on pulque maguey plantations in taking the plants from young shoots to the tapping stage are many. Stripped of their essentials, they are, in addition to several transplantings:[34]

(1) *Capazón.* When the central spine that surmounts the heart of the plant has turned black and thin, the plant has reached maturity, and the first step in the preparation of the central cavity is taken. The *capazón* procedure consists of removing the tight center cluster of modified leaves that acts as a protective sheath to the bud tip. A pointed pole is used for this purpose. After the bud tip is exposed, a few careful blows with the pole destroys completely the embryonic floral peduncle.

(2) *Picazón.* After *capazón*, the maguey is left alone for a period varying from several months to a year or more, during which the bud swells somewhat but does not grow vertically, since the incipient *quiote* has been destroyed. At the

appointed time, the *tlachiquero* punctures the entire surface of the top of the bud to a depth of several inches, using a sharp instrument. The mashed plant tissue is left in place for more than a week so that it will rot and be easily removed. This process creates both an irritation to the plant that stimulates the flow of sap and a cavity in which the sap may collect.

(3) *Raspa*. After the decayed material has been removed, the walls of the hole are carefully scraped. This rasping process removes the scar tissue that has formed, in order for the flow of sap into the cavity to continue unimpeded.

An early seventeenth-century account by Ruiz de Alarcon gives somewhat simpler procedures.[35] Transplanting is accomplished in plots containing rows of eight magueys each. *Capazón* and *picazón* are joined under the general name of *castración*, which is done with a strong, pointed pole. The procedure given by Ruiz is much more comprehensible on the basis of aboriginal techniques and ritualistic beliefs than the rather involved later process that separates the castration into two parts with a long period of waiting between them. It is also much more in line with our postulated invention of the pulque process through the cutting off of the *quiote*. Thus, with Ruiz the heart is removed immediately at maturity and the plant is tapped at once. This would reduce the total yield of sap, but would make for almost immediate availability. Probably there was some mystical association with (human) sacrifice in the sudden removal of the heart of the plant and the utilization of the discharge into the wound.[36] The *raspa* is accomplished with a spoon (*cuchara*) of copper. This instrument is undoubtedly aboriginal (called by Ruiz "*chichimeco vermejo*"), and is the precursor of the modern semiellipsoidal iron knife, *raspador*, for which Segura records the native name of *ocaxtle*.[37] A closely related word was probably the aboriginal Nahua name for the copper instrument.

Within a few days after the *raspa*, the maguey produces a steady flow of sap that continues without interruption until the plant is exhausted and the leaves have shrunk and collapsed into fibrous straps. The better pulque agaves yield during the few months of their tapping much more juice than the whole plant contains at any one time. A large specimen will yield from four to seven liters of sap daily over a period of three to six months; thus, a single plant will sometimes yield a total of more than 1,000 liters. The constant flow necessitates the removal of the aguamiel usually twice and occasionally three times daily. At each collection (*tlachicada*), the cavity, which in a large plant may be eighteen or twenty inches deep and ten to twelve inches in diameter, is scraped clean and a thin shaving is removed from the interior surface. The extraction is accomplished by means of a gourd pipette called "*acocote*" (*acocotli*, similar to the word used for the hollow cane described in note 37, this chapter), which is made from the dried, elongate fruit of the calabash, *Lagenaria vulgaris*.[38] An average-sized pipette will hold perhaps a liter.

Aguamiel is a turbid liquid having the appearance of greatly diluted milk. Occasionally, when extracted from the less desirable varieties of maguey, it has a yellowish or greenish cast. The odor of the freshly extracted sap is herbaceous, by no means unpleasant, and the taste is sweet, so that even the uninitiated generally find the drink agreeable. The percentage composition according to two series of analyses (apparently on liquids of different provenance) is as follows:[39]

	A	B
Density	*1.049*	*1.049*
Fixed acids [as H_2SO_4?]	0.068	0.069
Glucose	0.012	0.12
Sucrose	9.45	11.15
Gums	0.60	0.58
Albuminoids	0.806	0.81
Total solids	18.99	18.95
Ash	0.43	0.45

When aguamiel is allowed to stand for a few days it ferments and sours. To make pulque, a special procedure is followed in which the fresh sap is seeded by the addition of "mother of pulque" (*sinascle*, Nahuatl *xinachtli*), a culture containing the desired microorganisms. The sequence of steps followed nowadays in the fermentation of aguamiel on pulque haciendas and the very complicated microbiology involved[40] are beyond the scope of this discussion. Suffice it to point out that fermentation is most complex and that a number of different yeasts and bacteria play a part in it.

THE PROPERTIES OF PULQUE

Although aguamiel usually contains around 10 percent sucrose, only 3 or 4 percent alcohol is obtained in the fermented product, with the rest of the sugar converted into other oxidation products such as acetic acid and various gums. The gums and the viscid bacteria cultures give to old pulque its peculiar mucilaginous body, which in extreme cases is so pronounced that a finger dipped into the liquid will bring forth a milky scum like that of algae on a stagnant pond. An analysis of a typical fresh pulque gives about the following percentage composition:[41]

Density	*0.990 to 1.008*
Ethyl alcohol	3.72
Higher alcohols	0.00
Albuminoids	0.81
Gums	4.02
Unfermented sugar	1.80
Ash	0.64
Glycerine	0.09
Free acid [as H_2SO_4?]	0.18
Water	88.74
	100.00

The smell of pulque is distinctly *sui generis*. It is unmistakable, but impossible to describe. Human language is hopelessly rudimentary when it comes to olfactory vocabulary. Really fresh pulque does not have an objectionable odor. It is faintly reminiscent of bananas—in fact, "banana oil," evidently a concoction based on amyl acetate, has been added occasionally to stale pulque to return it to the original taste and smell.[42] Pulque should be consumed within a day after it is ready, for it quickly undergoes a putrescent decomposition and acquires a most objectionable stench. Gómara commented on this fact as early as 1552, saying: "There are no dead dogs, nor a bomb, than can clear a path as well as the smell of . . . this [wine]."[43] The odor seems to result from the action of microorganisms on the albuminoids in the pulque.[44]

The chemical composition of pulque, plus its being an active culture of yeasts and bacteria, appears to have two corollaries for those who consume it habitually in quantity: (1) It is a rich source of vitamin B_1.[45] (2) It may induce the formation of a beneficent colonic flora, and so play a role in keeping down the incidence of dysenteries and related diseases. In this regard it appears to act similarly to the well-known yogurt cultures in milk clabber.[46]

Even in pre-Columbian times, these factors must have been of considerable importance to the health and well-being of the inhabitants of the plateau, in particular to the urban population of the large towns and the underprivileged Otomí population in the north. Recent studies have indicated that the present submarginal dietary of these Indians makes the consumption of pulque a necessity, both for the sake of vitamins and for the caloric food value, not to mention its significance as a source of potable water in areas where water is scarce or badly contaminated.

The Pulque Roots

The aboriginal procedure in pulque manufacture almost invariably called for the addition of "pulque medicine." The tradition of its use was firmly ingrained and, according to the legend, its discovery was coeval with the discovery of pulque itself.[47] Immediately after the Conquest, when the native boundary lines had been broken and traditional restraints were no longer operative, inebriety increased to an alarming extent,[48] and the Spanish crown, in an effort to decrease the social demoralization of the natives, passed an edict prohibiting the use of "pulque root" in the manufacture of the beverage.[49] It is significant that the auxiliary herb, not the alcoholic drink itself, was prohibited. Evidently, the consultant to the Queen's council was convinced that the real evil lay in the effects of the root and not in the alcohol (his opinion undoubtedly had some truth to it). This royal edict of 1529, and subsequent reinforcements of the prohibition by the cabildo of Mexico City and by other decrees from 1545 on, caused the use of pulque roots to disappear in the neighborhood of the capital. But in remote places, the practice lived on; in Oaxaca, pulque is made to this day with pulque roots.

Two main varieties of pulque roots were used, both of them related to the *limacatlín* of the Totonac. They were not ordinarily planted, however, as the *cédula* of 1529 states, but were imported from the "hot lands" or "temperate lands."[50] In Oaxaca, they grew wild in moist places in the hills. Zimatlán, a town a few miles south of the city of Oaxaca, probably acquired the name because of the abundance there of the roots (from *çimatl*, "root," and *-tlan*, "place of").[51] The two roots were known in Nahuatl as *quauhpatli* (*quauitl*, "tree"; *patli*, "medicine" or "herb") and *ocpatli* (*octli*, "pulque"; *patli*). The Cuicatec name for *ocpatli* is *yacuaa*.[52] Among the post-Conquest names are *timbe, timbre, timbrillo, palo de pulque, canela*.[53] The taxonomic identification of these plants is difficult to determine since adequate collections have not been made and there is considerable confusion in the nomenclature. Not only is the same thing sometimes known under various names in different areas but also the same name often applies to different things. In the main, these pulque roots appear to be closely related species of Leguminosae, in particular of *Acacia* and *Calliandra*. Aguilar considers *quauhpatli* to be identical with *Acacia angustissima*, and his drawings of plant and leaves from the neighborhood of Zimatlán closely resemble herbarium specimens of this species I have seen.[54] Standley mentions that *Acacia angustissima* is called "*timbe*" and "*palo de pulque*" in Oaxaca and that its bark is used for tanning skins and for inducing fermentation in *tepache* (a drink of colonial origin of variable composition—in this case, a fermented mixture of pulque and brown sugar, with or without the addition of other ingredients). Standley also equates *Calliandra* with *timbrillo* and *canela*, and states: "The plant is sometimes used for tanning. The root is used to retard fermentation in a drink, 'tepache,' made from pulque and coarse sugar. The plant is said to contain a glucoside, calliandrine."[55] This species may be identifiable with one kind of *ocpatli*, although we have no certain information. A more technical discussion of the action of these substances is given in Appendix B.

Aguilar cites a document dated 1691 entitled "*Parecer y sentir acerca de las raices del ocpatli y del quapatli para fermentar el pulque, y si esta bebida es nociva o no lo es a la salud*," that was written by Ambrosio de la Lima y Escalada. I could not relocate this interesting account, which was some years ago in the possession of Nícolas León. Its principal conclusions seem to be that *guauhpatli* was used mainly around the Valley of Mexico and was favorable to the formation of good pulque and not harmful to the consumer, whereas *ocpatli* or *iztacuapatli* (*iztacquauhpatli*), which was employed mainly in the basin of Puebla, was harmful and had caused numerous deaths.[56] Lima y Escalada's *ocpatli* is definitely not *Calliandra anomala*, since the latter is deep red in color, and *iztacquauhpatli*, (*iztac*, "white"; *quauitl*, "tree"; *patli*, "herb"), his synonym for *ocpatli*, shows by its name that the color is not red.[57]

For the western part of the pre-Cortesian pulque region, there seems to be no record of the use of pulque roots. Their use is not mentioned in any of the *relaciones geográficas* of Michoacán or Nueva Galicia, whether early or late, nor are they recorded in other accounts that I have seen, with the one minor exception of a report from the eighteenth century. If they were used aboriginally at all, it is certain that their use was casual and sporadic rather than basic. The lesser degree of complexity of the pulque process in the west is additional evidence that the introduction came from the east.

The single exception mentioned above refers not to the true pulque roots *ocpatli* or *guauhpotl*, but rather to an herb called *tepopotl* (*Baccharis* sp.). Its Spanish name is *escoba* or *escobilla*, and the scrubby branches of various members of the genus are sometimes collected in Mexico and made into brooms. A report to the viceroy in 1787 mentions this herb as an ingredient in pulque in Michoacán, and states further that the plant is so poisonous that livestock die after eating it.[58] A report on prohibition compiled in 1692 by Joseph de la Barrera and referring apparently to the area around Mexico City mentions that *tepopotl* is the most poisonous of roots put into pulque.[59] Whether this root was a pre-Conquest ingredient is impossible to say—although, for Michoacán, it probably was not. We have no information as to whether the root was used alone or in conjunction with one of the traditional pulque roots discussed before.

Later Drinks Based on Pulque

In the colonial period, other ingredients found their way into pulque to give distinctive flavors or additional potency. One of these was the fruit of the so-called pepper tree, *Schinus molle*. This plant was apparently unknown in Mexico before the conquest of Peru. Its common sixteenth-century name in Nahuatl was *pelonquauitl* (*pelon*, "Peru"[60]; *quauitl*, "tree"), which would indicate a Spanish introduction. The name "*copalquauitl*" (*copal*, "incense") was sometimes applied to these trees, but no significance can be attached to this, since the name was a generic term applicable to any tree that exuded a fragrant resin. According to a hoary tradition, Viceroy Mendoza sent some seeds of the plant to Mexico after his transfer to Peru in 1550. It may be so, although no documentary proof seems to have been found. Francisco Hernández does not mention Mendoza in his description of the tree, though he was a painstaking worker and present in the area within two decades after Mendoza's transfer.[61] More probably, *Schinus molle* was introduced into Mexico at some time in the early 1540s when there was a fair amount of contact between the two regions.

In Peru, honey, wine, and vinegar were made from the seeds of this tree, as Cieza de Leon testifies.[62] Garcilaso de la Vega gives the details regarding the wine as follows:

> The seed when ripe has on the surface a little sweetness which is very tasty and pleasant, but beyond that the rest is very bitter. They make a drink from that seed by rubbing it gently between the hands in hot water, until it has yielded all its sweetness. They must not arrive at the bitter portion, for otherwise all is spoiled. They pass that water through a sieve and let it stand for three or four days until it is ready [i.e., has fermented]. It is very good to drink, very tasty, and very healthful. . . . Mixed with the maize drink [a kind of *tesgüino*] it improves it and makes it more palatable.[63]

In Mexico, a pure *Schinus* wine is unknown, but the pleasant modifying influence of the seed on the taste of pulque when fermented in aguamiel was widely appreciated. The resultant beverage was known as *copaloctli*, a drink that did not become well established until the seventeenth century. It is not mentioned in the *relaciones geográficas* of the 1579 series, but later became the object of specific prohibition legislation. In the *relaciones* of 1777[64] and in the Navarro account of 1784,[65] the drink is listed for a number of places on the Mesa Central and in Oaxaca. The use of the seeds in cornstalk wine to give *"quebrantahuesos"* was mentioned earlier.

Chilocle (*Chiloctli*) is another modified pulque that was not known by the earlier chroniclers, but is mentioned subsequently. Its recipe, according to Navarro, calls for pulque, *chile ancho* (the large, mild chile), *pazote* (saltwort), garlic, and a pinch of salt.[66] It was used mainly on the Mesa Central, and its distribution falls largely into a triangular area whose vertices are Toluca, Ixmiquilpan, and Zacatlan. An outstanding exception outside this area is the town of Acapulco, where the drink is also found. In this case, the use of real pulque was out of the question, and the drink must have been made from the so-called *pulque amarillo* (see below).

The Navarro report gives an impressive list of other variations on the general theme of pulque.[67] Most of these are obviously of colonial origin:

Charape: pulque with an admixture of sugar, cinnamon, cloves, and anis.

Chinguirito: diluted maguey syrup fermented and distilled.

Coyote: low-grade pulque fermented with maguey syrup and *palo de timbre*.

Mezcal de pulque: *tlachique* fermented with sugarcane molasses and distilled.

Oztotzi: cornstalk juice and pulque fermented with *palo de timbre* (apparently aboriginal).

Polla Ronca: pulque flavored with blackberry, *capulin*, black pepper, and sugar.

Ponche de pulque: pulque with addition of aguardiente, cloves, and nutmeg.

Pulque de almendra: pulque with sugar and ground almond.

Pulque de atole: pulque with soured atole (maize gruel), strained and sweetened.

Pulque de durango: skinned peaches boiled to a jam, cooled, pulque and sugar added.

Pulque de guayaba: guayabas skinned and mashed, pulque and sugar added, strained.

Pulque de huevo: whites of egg beaten with pulque, sugar added.

Pulque de naranja: orange juice mixed with pulque.

Pulque de obos: obos (*Spondias* sp.) mashed in pulque, strained, and sugar added.

Pulque de piña: pineapples without the rind, mashed in pulque, strained, and sugar added.

Sangre de conejo: pulque fermented with juice and pulp of the *tapon nopal*, and strained. (Apparently aboriginal. The name, "rabbit's blood," refers to both its color and intoxicating potency. "Rabbit" is undoubtedly an allusion to the rabbit god of drink, *Ometochtli*.)

Tepache: pulque mixed with molasses and boiled with anis.

Tepache comun: the sediment of *pulque tlachique* fermented in water with maguey syrup, black pepper, and a maize leaf.

Tolonce: fruit of Peruvian pepper tree fermented in pulque [same as *copaloctli*?].

Pulque from Maguey Syrup

Maguey syrup, *menecutli* (*metl*, "agave"; *necutli*, "honey") was widely used in the pulque area. Its presence in the marketplace of Tenochtitlán was mentioned by Cortés in his second letter, and its importance in pre-Columbian Mexico as tribute to the Aztec rulers is graphically shown in the *Codex Mendocino*.[68] In addition to its use as food, this syrup was occasionally diluted with water and fermented into a kind of pulque, *aoctli* (*atl*, "water"; *octli*, "wine"), which because of the yellow color derived from the dark syrup became known in colonial times as *pulque amarillo*.[69] This beverage had two advantages: (1) It could be made beyond the limits of the pulque region since the syrup could be transported without spoiling, and (2) it could be made somewhat stronger than ordinary pulque because the fermentation could be started in a liquid of higher sugar content than was contained in the aguamiel. Usually, pulque roots were added.

The aboriginal distribution of *aoctli* is very imperfectly recorded. It was certainly used in a place like Cuicatlán, Oaxaca, which is situated in a deep canyon at the very edge of the pulque region, and in some other locations of similar peripheral character. For Tepoztlán, Xalapa, and Pánuco, however, we know definitely from the *relaciones* of the 1580 series that pulque was made directly from aguamiel.[70] On the plateau, *octli* and *aoctli* were both used.[71] The *relación geográfica* for Cuauhquilpan of 1581 relates that the inhabitants made pulque directly from aguamiel and also from the boiled-down syrup, but that it was not so good.[72] Evidently *pulque amarillo* was usually made somewhat stronger than ordinary pulque, for the Spanish officials considered it very harmful, and prohibitions against it were in effect from 1570 on.[73]

Terminology

Much has been written concerning the origin of the word "pulque." The Nahua equivalent was *octli* or *uctli*; and it is certain that "pulque" was not used aboriginally in Mexico. Clavigero suggests that the Spaniards brought the word with them from Chile, where "*púlcu*" is the Araucanian term for fermented drinks.[74] There are two objections to that argument: first, *púlcu* in Chile referred to maize chicha and not to maguey wine, which was unknown there,[75] and second, the word "pulque" was in common use in Mexico long before the Spaniards had any contact with the Araucanians.[76]

Wiener has attempted to derive the word "*pulquería*" (pulque shop), and by extension the word "pulque," from the Spanish "*pulpería*," which, according to Costa Alvarez, is "a store in the Indies where various kinds of goods are sold, such as wine, brandy or liquors, drugs, peddlers' wares, notions, and others; but not cloth, canvas, or other woven materials."[77] It seems, however, that *pulpería* is a word of colonial Peruvian derivation, and hence was later in appearance than the other. García Icazbalceta quotes the Inca Garcilaso as claiming that the word *"pulpero"* (one who owns a *pulpería*) is applied to the poorest merchants in Peru because in the store of one of them a *pulpo* (cuttlefish) was found on sale.[78] Even if it were true, as Wiener appears to believe, that *"pulpero"* has its roots in Old Spanish, we should still have to explain the sudden and immediate appearance of the words *"pulquero"* and *"pulque"* in Mexico. There is not the least indication of a prior use of *pulpero*, nor of the occurrence of a similar linguistic mutation in other areas. The real etymology seems to be tied up regionally with the pulque area itself.

Knowing the diffidence with which the Spaniards approached the problem of nomenclature in the New World, a few linguists have examined the etymology of "pulque" from the standpoint of a possible Spanish modification of some Nahua term. According to Nuñez Ortega, the word is derived from *"poliuhqui uctli"* (decomposed wine) by a process of contraction and elision.[79] The intermediate form *"poliúctli"* may have been conceived and pronounced by some of the Spaniards as *"pulcre."* By a process of further simplification, mainly because the natives could not pronounce the letter 'r,' the term "pulque" finally became standardized. Robelo himself believes that the explanation need not begin with anything so cumbersome as *poliuhqui uctli*. He plausibly argues that the vendors of the beverage must frequently have used the word *"poliuhqui"* in referring to the matter of the liquid spoiling in twenty-four or thirty-six hours; the Spaniards must have overheard them and thought that the term referred to the drink in general rather than to its decomposed state.[80]

In addition to *"octli,"* pulque had another aboriginal Nahua name: *"neuctli."* Plancarte y Navarrete explains that *"octli"* was the term for the ordinary run of pulque, while *"neuctli"* was used to refer to the finest variety.[81] Even today, *"neuctli"* is in use in certain parts when Mexicano is spoken. I found it used at Milpa Alta, D.F., in 1938. The word *"tlachique"* was applied to the poorest grade of pulque or to aguamiel that had not yet fermented sufficiently to be considered *octli*. According to Robelo, the word is derived from the verb *"tla chiqui,"* meaning "to scrape," and refers to the rasping of the cavity in the maguey plant during the tapping process.[82] Finally, there is the word *"tepache,"* whose meaning is rather indefinite, but which applies to a number of drinks that have been artificially sweetened and then fermented. *Tepache de pulque* is a beverage prepared by fermenting a mixture of pulque and syrup or sugar, with or without the addition of other ingredients; *tepache de piña* is made by fermenting mashed pineapples in a syrup or sugar solution, etc. The word *"tepache"* is said to be derived from the

Nahua term "*tepacho*," meaning "chieftain or leader," in ironic allusion to the self-important verbosity it arouses in some people when consumed to excess.[83]

LESSER DRINKS IN THE PULQUE REGION

Pulque and its derivatives were culturally of such over-whelming importance in the pulque region that other beverages held only a minor place. They did exist, however, and they became increasingly significant toward the peripheries of the region. The fundamental position of mescal wine has already been discussed. It is entirely probable that this beverage, the histori-cal if not the technological precursor of pulque, was still being made in the early sixteenth century in places remote from the northeastern center of the pulque complex's origin (i.e., in places where pulque can be considered a relatively recent intrusion). The areas in which mescal brandy was soon to assume a posi-tion of importance—for example, northwestern Jalisco (around Tequila) and central Oaxaca—almost certainly had an unbroken tradition of baking and fer-menting mescal. Likewise, the understory of *tesgüino* and cornstalk wine was established for the northern fringes of the pulque area. In this connection the dictionary of Molina furnishes a useful list:[84]

(1) "*Tlaoloctli*; *teuhoctli* — Wine of wheat or maize." Wheat is of course a Spanish introduction. Hence, these two Nahuatl terms refer to corn beer and can be considered the specific Nahua names for *tesgüino*. Since the word "*tes-güino*" is derived from "*teiuinti*," a general term for something intoxicating, that word would obviously be inadequate in an area where the basic drink was pulque. *Octli* is the usual word for wine or beer; *tlaolli* means maize kernels; *teuhtli* is the word for dust or powder; and Siméon finds himself unable to explain adequately the etymology of *teuhoctli*.[85] Perhaps it is meant to refer to the common gritty character of corn beer, the result of many hours of boiling in open pots over a wood fire. The sample of *tesgüino* I tasted among the Huichol had every right to claim the appellation of "gritty beer."

(2) "*Xoco octli* — Wine of plums or lemons." Lemons and true plums were brought from Europe, but the word "*ciruela*" was used by the Spaniards for the various members of the genus *Spondias*, known in English as "hog plums."[86] These American "plums" occurred in many varieties, though Standley lists only two species, *S. purpurea* and *S. mombin*.[87] The Nahuatl name for *Spondias* sp. was *xocotl*, the generic name for acidulous fruit, of which these were considered the prototype.[88] The word was changed to *xocoge* and *jocote* by the Spaniards, and these names have remained. From the Antilles, the term "*jobo*" ("*hobo*," "*obo*") was introduced, which also has a wide distribution today. Sahagún lists a number of specific terms for "*xocotl*," among which are *téxocotl* (*tetl*, "rock"),

described as being red or yellow *manzanillas* with little seeds inside (*Crataegus mexicana*); *mazaxocotl* (*mazatl*, "deer"), red or yellow ciruelas of various sizes, from the hot country (evidently *Spondias purpurea*); *atoyatl* ("stream"), big, sweet and tasty ciruelas from which wine is made (also *S. purpurea*); and *xalxocotl* (*xalli*, "sand"), fruit with yellow or dark green skin, and white, pink, or red pulp containing many seeds (evidently the guayaba, *Psidium guajava*).[89] Obviously only his "deer plum" and "stream plum" are *Spondias*. Hernandez adds three other species to the Nahua genus *xocotl*. They are *copalxocotl* (*copal*, "resin"), yellow, edible fruit with resinous flesh and acid flavor (*Cyrtocarpa procera*); *mexocotl* (*metl*, "agave"), plant with leaf habit of maguey or pineapple bearing sweet-sour fruit like ciruelas (*Bromelia karatas* and *B. pinguin*, equivalent to the plants called *xococuistle, jocuiste, aguámara, aguama, timbiriche, piñuela*, etc.); and *guauhxocotl* (*quauitl*, "tree"), also called *xocoyolli*, plants belonging to the sorrel family (*Oxalis* sp.).[90] Of these three, none belongs to the *Spondias* genus, though *Cyrtocarpa* is closely related.

Hog plums have a wide distribution in the American tropics, and they are typically plants of the *Aw* climate.[91] (See Figure 19.) Rarely do they overlap the edges of the pulque region. Among the places in the pulque area for which *Spondias* wine is mentioned in the 1579 *relaciones* are Papaloticpac, Atlatlauaca y Malinaltepec, and Cuicatlán.[92] All three lie on the extreme fringes of the pulque lands and are transitional in character.

As to the character of hog-plum wine, Sahagún remarks somewhat enigmatically: "They make this pulque more to drink and get drunk than for the syrup."[93] Further information regarding the utilization of *Spondias* for wine in the warmer lands is in chapter 8.

(3) "*Matzaoctli* — Wine from pineapples." Pineapple wine was a beverage of purely tropical distribution and is discussed in chapter 9.

(4) "*Capuloctli* — Wine from cherries." The significant root in the name of the beverage is "*capulín*," a Nahuatl word that is difficult to define. In general it has reference to small fruits, usually but not invariably edible, that fall neither into the category of the larger acidulous fruits known as "*xocotl*" nor into the group of large, sweet, often rather insipid-tasting fruits known collectively as "*tzapotl*." The *capulín* group contains many genera in the modern taxonomic sense. For all of Mexico, Martínez lists fourteen genera, each of which contains at least one species known as "*capulín*" in some part of the country, and six other genera with component species called "*capulincillo*," the hispanicized diminutive.[94] The only *capulines* that are definitely known to have been fermented for wine are true cherries, members of the genus *Prunus*, and in particular *P. capuli*.

Figure 19. A Huichol youth beside a dormant ciruelo, or hog plum (*Spondias* sp.), demonstrating the use of bow and arrow.

Prunus capuli is native to moderate and cold zones, ranging in altitude from 4,000 to 10,000 feet. Lowland varieties and, possibly, closely related species also occur. The taxonomy even of the economic *capulines* belonging to the genus *Prunus* is difficult, partly because not enough collections have been made from the economic point of view and partly because varietal differences have become fixed in many areas through centuries of selection and cultivation. The aboriginal range of *P. capuli* extended from somewhere around the Tropic of Cancer southward an unknown distance into Central America, but did not include Yucatán. It is now found growing wild in the mountains of northwestern South America, but its occurrence there probably stems from a colonial introduction and subsequent escape.[95]

On some parts of the Mexican plateau, *P. capuli* was very abundant at the time of the Conquest. Cortés wrote in his third letter, dated Cuyoacan, May 15, 1522:

[A]ll our native allies are lodged at Cuyoacan about a league and a half away, and both this town and others provided us with certain supplies of which we were in great want, especially fish and cherries [*cerezas*], which are so abundant that they would do for twice as many people as there are in this land during the five or six months in which they are in season.[96]

Of the sixteenth-century *relaciones* published by Paso y Troncoso, fully two dozen mention the occurrence of *capulín*, but not one mentions utilization for wine.[97] Sahagún does not mention the wine either, which may be regarded as evidence that the beverage was rarely if ever made around Mexico City. Ximénez, however, observes that the fruit is used for food and wine in times of scarcity, but he gives no regional localization.[98]

A field trip into Puebla and Veracruz in 1939 brought to light the fact that *capulín* wine is still made by some of the Totonac living in the mountains at intermediate elevations. The following list of *capulín* varieties was obtained from a consultant in Zongozotla, Puebla. The first four are probably *Prunus capuli*, the fifth probably not, and the last named is certainly a different genus. Fermentation for wine is recorded only for the first two.

(1) *Huitzitzíqui* — Small tree, about three meters high, bearing sweet black cherries of small size. It grows especially in the hills around Tetela, Puebla, where an excellent dark red wine called "*huiquiño*" is made from the fruit.

(2) *Elocapuli*[99] — A tree eight to ten meters high. From the fruit, which is good-sized, a wine is made around Huahuaxtla, Puebla.

(3) *Capulín grande* — Also known as *ombligo de virga*(?).

(4) *Niguilla* — Shrub or small tree, two meters high. Very sweet fruit. Cultivated in Zongozotla, Puebla. The Totonac name is "*mojút*."

(5) *Xalcápuli* — *Capulin arenoso* ("sand cherry"). Grows near Cuetzalan, Puebla, and at still lower elevations toward the coast.

(6) *Tchatáya* (Totonac name) — Spiny tree. Fruit used only for medicine.

Martínez lists under *Prunus capuli* an ordinary form, *capulín*; a light-colored form, *capulín blanco*; and a bitter astringent form, *capulín cimarron* or *capulí del cerro*. For a sweet variety, he records an analysis showing about 19 percent total sugar.[100]

EIGHT

Mescal and Jocote

West of the lands of *tesgüino* and pulque and south of the northwest cactus region there lies a long lowland strip in which aboriginal alcoholic drinks were derived mainly from mescal and jocote (*Spondias purpurea*). In the north, the area goes as far as the aboriginal limits of higher culture around Culiacan, and in the south, it has an obscure boundary somewhere around the lower Balsas drainage. The boundaries of the region are in the main cultural, although the limits of the pulque region are determined largely by the extent to which pulque agaves descend toward the coast. For the most part, the area is *Aw* in climate, although it crosses the *BS* boundary in the north and the *Cw* boundary in the realm of the Cora. These climatic boundaries have little significance in the present instance, since both mescal and jocote distributions cut across them.

The northern frontier was occupied by the Tahue. For them we have early records of the wide use of mescal wine and of wine from "ciruelas."[1] The Totorame farther south were decimated so completely by the Guzman's conquest that ethnologic data are extremely scanty. No statement regarding alcoholic beverages has been located. Their relatives and partial descendants to the east, the Cora, utilize several different kinds of mescal agave for food and drink, as well as *jocuistle* (*Bromelia* sp.) and possibly *Spondias*, and we may assume that the Totorame had similar drinks. (See Map 2 in chapter 2.)

To include the Cora in this essentially lowland region is not so anomalous as it appears at first glance, since many of the Cora settlements are in deep canyons where true *Aw* climate prevails, and, as mentioned, linguistic and cultural ties link the Cora country to the higher culture of the coastal plains.[2] Cultural differences between the Cora and their near neighbors in the *tesgüino* region, the Huichol, are still fairly great, and were probably much more marked aboriginally.

In the *relación geográfica* of 1777 for the Cora mission (Jesús María y José) is the following list of plants used to make alcoholic drinks:[3]

Plants with which they make wine.
Mescals that also are used to make many medicines.
Tepemet
Mascarillo
Chocohuite is also eaten, and also has fresh sap that
    everyone knows how to turn into a wine as spirited as
    the brandy of Spain.
Also there are some pulque magueys.

Tepemet (*tepemetl,* "mountain agave") and *mascarillo* (evidently for *mescalillo*) are both forms of mescal. The *relación* records the use of their *quiotes* for food. *Chocohuite* (in Nahuatl, *Xoxoicxitl,* "fruit stalk," or *mexocotl,* "agave fruit") refers to two nonepiphytic bromelias (*Bromelia karatas* and *B. pinguin*) that grow wild in many parts of the hot and moderate zones of Mexico and Central America.[4] They go under a great many different names in various regions, some of which have been listed in the text of chapter 7 in connection with notes 89 and 90. The statement about "*vino*"-like aguardiente in connection with *chocohuite* shows that distillation was practiced. The art of distillation had probably been in the area for a century and a half when the *relación* was written. The spread of pulque magueys has already been discussed. The fermentation of *Spondias* is nowhere expressly recorded for the Cora, but the 1777 *relación* for the mission San Ygnacio de Huainamota mentions the presence of "ciruelos." This account states further that mescales were used for fiber and "*vino*" and that they were both wild and planted.[5] The chances are that this planting was not aboriginal but was a direct result of the introduction of distillation. (Figure 20.)

    The linguistic situation in western Jalisco is highly complicated, but culture as expressed by the presence of intoxicating beverages is strikingly uniform. The 1579 *relación* for Tenemaztlán mentions much drunkenness among the natives. It does not go into details regarding their beverages, but lists several kinds of "*sirguelas*" (*Spondias*).[6] For Autlán, on the edge of the pulque region, the *relación* of 1777 gives a number of mescal varieties from which brandy is obtained, including *mescal manzo, gualampo, lechuguilla,* and *tecolote.*[7] The last three are said to be of inferior grade. *Mescal de Autlán* is still made today and probably harkens back, as is the case with practically all modern mescal distilling, to the aboriginal use of mescal wine. For the nearby town of Tuscaquesco (Tuxcacuesco), the *relación* for 1579 mentions wine from jocote (*Spondias*), as does also the 1579 *relación* for Zapotitlán.[8] The latter lies at the edge of the aboriginal pulque region. Wine from jocote is rarely made in this general area today, but in the marketplace of many of the towns, at least as far inland as Sayula, a large red hog plum is sold in late

Figure 20. Henry Bruman with ethnologist/photographer Bodil Christiansen in the Jalisco-Nayarit border country, 1938.

spring and early summer under the name of "*ciruela borrachera.*" Undoubtedly this fruit was once fermented.

In the vicinity of Colima, it is difficult to reconstruct the aboriginal drink picture. The 1579 *relación* has not been located; and by the end of the sixteenth century, an entirely extraneous development, the manufacture of brandy from coconut-palm wine, had pushed into the background the indigenous intoxicants. Of native drinks the exceedingly detailed Tecalitan *relación* of 1789 has nothing to say, while the Ystlahuacan (Ixtlahuacan) account of 1778 mentions only mescal. In the latter report, the great abundance of wild grapes in the hills is commented upon and the opinion expressed that brandy from these grapes might be less harmful than mescal.[9] From that statement we infer the *Vitis* was not used aboriginally for wine.[10] A local variety of hog plum, known as "*ciruela de Mispan,*" is planted in southern Colima. This may have been the *ciruela* mentioned in the Motín *relación* of 1589.[11] Motín was located southeast of the mouth of the Coahuayana River in territory now belonging to Michoacán. "*Vino de maguey*" is also mentioned. If this was pulque, the account must have referred to the hill country north of Motín since the town lay outside the pulque region. Just west of the lower Balsas lived another group of lowland Nahua. They are included in the mescal and jocote region by virtue of an analogy with the not-distant Nahua of Colima. Beyond Zacatula, the problem becomes more difficult, and no reliable limits can be drawn, although around the great elbow bend of the Balsas and upstream for some distance, the mescal and jocote region appears to have extended to the limits of pulque. The eastern portion of the great enclosed *Aw* basin of the Balsas drainage is outside the area, where honey wine (mead) assumes a position of dominance.

NINE

The Region beyond Mescal

In the lowlands east and south of the pulque region, the aboriginal drink picture becomes suddenly much more complicated. It is at present impossible to delineate valid drink regions as clearly as they are in the preceding chapters for northern and central Mexico. The reasons for the difficulty are in part our fragmentary knowledge of the aboriginal ethnology of many areas, aggravated by the extreme, historic shattering of linguistic and cultural units over much of Central America, but even more so in the intrinsic complexity of the drink picture itself. Only in one area, that of the Maya and the Lacandón, can a region be logically indicated, and even there the southern limits are conjectural.

Individual kinds of drinks had a most spotty distribution. Thus, pineapple wine (*matzaoctli* in Nahuatl) had a great importance in the pineapple area (Matzatlan) in northern Oaxaca, was apparently used also by the Nahua of southern Morelos and eastern Guerrero, was somewhat significant among the Lacandón, and appears again and again in many parts of Central America and northern South America in a varied company of other drinks.

Palm wine, if it is indeed aboriginal in the New World (see note 15, this chapter), represents a similar case. It has already been cited for the Huaxtec; it is known among the lowland Nahua of Veracruz and Soconusco; and it occurs in many parts to the south. If the origin of this wine is connected with an aboriginal utilization of the palm cabbage for food, then it may have been known even along the Pacific slopes of Jalisco and Nayarit. The coyol palm (*Acrocomia mexicana*) and the coquito (*Orbignya cohune*) are undoubtedly aboriginal in this area, and the use of the cabbage of two or three kinds of palms for food is mentioned in the Tenamaztlán (Jalisco) *relación* of 1579.[1]

Similar wide and sporadic distributions occurred for beers from sprouted or chewed maize, which were highly important as far south as Peru, and for wines made from jocote (*Spondias*) and *jocuistle* (*Bromelia*). Beverages that were typical of the drier lands of Mexico had little or no importance east of Tehuántepec. Among these were pulque, which appears to have been quite unknown beyond the limits indicated on the map in chapter 7; mescal wine, which at best played only a very minor role in Chiapas and Guatemala, and may have been quite unknown; cactus wines; and mesquite wines.

THE LANDS WEST OF THE MAYA AND QUICHÉ

Southeast of the mescal and jocote region lay an area in which honey played an important role in native economy. The *Codex Mendocino* gives a list of twenty towns, mostly in Morelos and eastern Guerrero, which paid honey as tribute to the Aztec rulers.[2] For the Tlapanec, we have a definite statement that they made a native wine from honey and the roots of herbs.[3] Schultze-Jena reported a beer from sprouted maize and sugarcane molasses in use among the Tlapanec a few years ago.[4] It is likely that the recipe called for sprouted maize and honey aboriginally, unless cornstalk syrup was used in place of the honey. (See Map 10.)

The 1580 *relación* of Citlaltomagua y Anecuilco presents some interesting problems.[5] These settlements were located in the hills a few miles northwest of Acapulco and, according to the account, paid placer gold as tribute to the Aztecs in pre-Conquest times. The language was Tepuztec [Tepetixtec?]. These Indians were accomplished drunkards, for the *relación* reads:

> They made good use of cornstalks, pineapples, bananas, and hog plums to make much pulque or wine which accounted for their drunkenness, and they would become very intoxicated in the cantina, where there were many injuries and much sickness from which they would pass out on the floor . . . and would remain constantly drunk for more than ten days. They make another wine from certain magueys, but that wine is not as devastating as the pulques they make.[5]

On this basis, then, we can list wines from cornstalks, pineapples, bananas (plaintains?)[6], hog plums, and agave.[7]

The Amuzgo near the Guerrero-Oaxaca border were said to be much given to drunkenness,[8] but no reliable account of their beverages has been seen. Among the Zapotec of the lowlands of southern Oaxaca, a beverage with intoxicating qualities was made from *xocoyolle* (*Oxalis* sp.).[9] This plant of the sorrel family, which seems to be identical with Hernandez's *quauhxocotl*,[10] bears a small carrot-shaped root perhaps three inches long and three-quarters of an inch in diameter near the top. The *relaciones* of 1777 for Coatlan and Guijecollani in southern Oaxaca mention that the Indians of the neighborhood (Zapotec) commonly

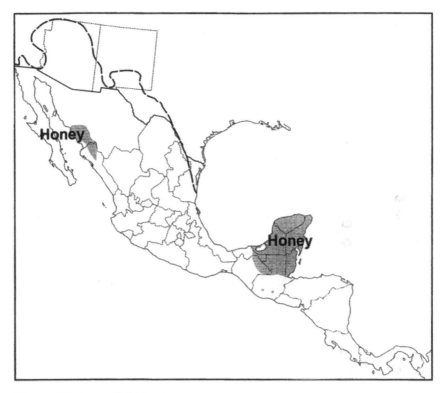

Map 10. The honey/*balché* regions.

became intoxicated with it.[11] The plant is recorded for other areas—for example, Ystlachucán (Colima) and San Miguel el Grande (Hidalgo)—but only in the southern Zapotec area is an intoxicating drink mentioned. How the drink is made and whether it intoxicates because of alcohol or alkaloids is not recorded.

No trustworthy information about the kinds of alcoholic drinks used by the members of the Zoque linguistic family (Mixe, Huave, Popoloca of Veracruz, and Zoque) has come to hand. In the Chinantla, the lowlands just north of the Zapoteca, at least three aboriginal wines were made.[12] They included beverages from pineapple, from mamey (*Calocarpum mammosum*), and from "*hobos*" (*Spondias* sp., perhaps *S. mombin*). Use of the root of a small tree called "*tepesi-matl*" (*tepetl*, "hill"; *cimatl*, "root") as an auxiliary herb is recorded also. The plant may be identical with one of the so-called pulque roots of the Zapoteca. Adjacent to the Chinantec on the northwest lived the Matzatec, named after their main settlement, Matzatlán. The 1579 *relación* for Matzatlán mentions much drunkenness, but the beverages are not specified.[13] We can be confident, however, that pineapple wine was one of them, quite possibly the main one.

Much of the Gulf lowlands belongs in this area of miscellaneous tropical beverages. The use of coyol palm wine has already been mentioned for the Huaxteca. A fermented drink of lesser importance among the lowland Huaxteca appears to be wine from the "soursop" or guanabana (*Annona muricata*). For the highland Totonac, cornstalk wine and capulin wine have been cited previously. The lowland Totonac around Papantla make a *tepache de piña* today from pineapples and sugarcane juice. Aboriginally they probably used cornstalk juice or honey in place of the latter. Honey is plentiful in the area. A beverage of low alcoholic content is made by fermenting the root of the sarsaparilla (*Smilax medica*), which is native to the region. The result is somewhat reminiscent of root beer, and is still sold on Sundays and feast days in the markets of Papantla. Hogplum wine appears to be unknown.

Palm wine is recorded for the Nahua population of southern Veracruz. The 1777 *relación* of Chacaltianguiz, a town located along the lower course of the Papaloapan River, states:

> There are two species of palm, the one with the shape of the date palm is the real palm and the other is the local palm; the difference is the real one is larger and its fruit is called "*collol*," and from the heads of these palms they make a wine in the same way as that from the maguey.[14]

This "*collol*" seems to be *Orbignya cohune*.

It is significant that the author of this *relación* comments on making a wine similar to the pulque process. Evidently, then, the local procedure was to let the tree stand, cut out the palmito or a part of it, and collect the juices that seeped into the hole.

The Nahua of southwestern Chiapas likewise knew coyol wine. Their method, however, as told to me in Chiapas by people who had witnessed it, was to fell a tall palm and to carve out a hole with one or two liters' capacity near the top end of the reclining trunk. The flow of sap would continue for a week or two. The sap, which was withdrawn once or twice a day, was consumed when it was judged sufficiently fermented. The Lacandón chop off the trunk of the palm, leaving a four-foot stump standing above the ground. A hole, a foot wide and two feet deep, is excavated in the top of the stump and is stopped up with bark and sticks to protect the juice from contamination by rain and from loss by animals drinking it. The flow lasts about a week and sap is removed two or three times a day. The usual period of fermentation is seventy-two hours. This process is both novel and wasteful, since the juice in the main part of the trunk seems to go unutilized. According to the consultant, the Lacandón use the Spanish word "*taberna*" to designate palm wine.[15]

One of the truly indigenous beverages of Chiapas is a beer from sprouted maize brewed with the addition of the inner bark of a certain tree. The bark appears in the markets of the Chiapas highlands in small skeins composed of long and narrow, pliable strips called "*mecate*" (from the Nahuatl *mecatl*, "cord") and is used mainly for tying bundles. The variety known as *mecate colorado* is generally used in the beverage. In Tzotzil, this bark is known as *tzoj ak*; in Tzeltal, as *chanján*; and in Mexicano, as *majagua*. Its use is especially prevalent around Simojovel and Panteló. No other parts of a *mecate* plant were seen, and a sample of bark that was brought back for analysis could not be identified botanically. Judging from the name "*majagua*" and its utilization for cordage, the plant is probably either a *Hibiscus* or *Heliocarpus*.

The only other fermented drinks of the Chiapas highlands that could be determined are of colonial origin: pulque among the Tzotzil of Chamula, as mentioned before, and so-called chicha of sugarcane juice, which now has wide distribution.[16]

THE BALCHÉ REGION

Among the Maya and some of their close relatives to the south, a very characteristic alcoholic drink was made by fermenting diluted honey with the bark of the *balché* (*Lonchocarpus longistylus*). Mead was an aboriginal beverage in several parts of the New World (Sinaloa and eastern Guerrero have already been mentioned), but nowhere else was the *balché* bark used as an additional and invariable ingredient. In Yucatán, this bark and honey beverage, which was also called "*balché*," appears to have had no competitors; all the evidence seems to indicate that it was the only alcoholic intoxicant of the true Maya at the time of the Conquest.[17]

The gathering of honey from wild and partially domesticated bees was one of the main activities of the aboriginal Maya. All of the early accounts, in particular those of Landa and López de Médel,[18] as well as the *relaciones geográficas* of the 1579 series,[19] are eloquent on the great significance of bees and of the *balché* drink in the economic and ritual life of the Maya. Recent studies by Sapper have shed much light on beekeeping in this area, and on the related industries.[20] Native American bees are stingless, and some varieties were partially domesticated by the Maya and kept in small hives in or near the huts,[21] which was apparently also the case among some of the tribes with a more complex culture along the west coast. Other varieties lived wild in the woods, and the wax and honey from their nests were appropriated by the Indians whenever found.

One of the most informative of the *relaciones* of Yucatán relates the following about *balché*:

> Before the Spanish invasion, the Indians had happiness and great contentment, always going to fiestas, dances, and weddings, and making a wine from maguey sap and a root they called "*balché*" in their language. And they fermented it in a large wooden trough that held thirty or forty or fifty measures of liquid and boiled it only two days until it became potent and smelled bad. And at their dances, they dance after drinking repeatedly from small jars and in a short time become intoxicated and act as if they were crazy and childish. And I see much drunkenness like this.[22]

In the *relación* for Mérida the addition of maguey root to the other ingredients is mentioned,[23] but this procedure seems not to be recorded anywhere else. Even if the statement is based on accurate observation, it does not imply baking mescal, but most likely merely the addition of fresh agave root (see Appendix B). In the *relaciones* for Hocaba and Cotuto y Tibolon the recipe for *balché* is amended to include ground maize.[24] According to Tozzer, *balché* is "milky white, sour to the smell, and at first very disagreeable to the taste."[25]

A Spanish name for the beverage occasionally found in the literature is "*pitar-illa*."[26] It appears to be an old term of rather indefinite meaning, for a variant, "*pitarrillos*," is found in a letter written from the Philippines to the King of Spain by Mirandaola in 1574.[27]

Not only the Maya, but also the Lacandón, make *balché*. They frequently add maize to the brew, and nowadays sugarcane juice frequently replaces the traditional honey. According to Soustelle the fermenting vat is "the trunk of a tree hollowed out in the shape of a canoe." The fermentation takes place as follows: "The ground maize, the water, and the cornstalk juice and *balché* are put in the hollowed-out trunk. And after one night of fermentation the liquid is alcohol. One leaves it for two days if one wants to have a *balché* that is very intoxicating."[28]

The Lacandón, although they still belong in the *balché* culture area, must be considered as transitional, since they have a number of other alcoholic beverages. Their use of palm-stem wine has already been mentioned, although this beverage, as indicated, may not be aboriginal. Pineapple wine seems to be truly indigenous, however. It is mentioned in a missionary letter as early as 1695.[29] It may even be that an aboriginal area of pineapple wine extended from the Matzatec, Cuicatec, and Chinantec eastward across the Isthmus of Tehuántepec as far as the Petén. Other indigenous beverages among the Lacandón, according to the competent consultant from Ococingo already quoted in connection with *taberna*, are made from *piñuela* (*Bromelia* sp.) and from the fruit of the *chicoza-pote* (*Achras*).[30] *Chicozapote* wine has been encountered nowhere else.

Resume of Central-American Beverages

The southern limits of the aboriginal *balché* region cannot be definitely drawn for the reason that sugarcane arrived very early in the lands of the southern tribes of Mayance languages (Quiché, Kekchi, Cakchiquel, etc.) and effectively replaced the earlier honey and/or cornstalk juice in the preparation of fermented drinks. A comparison of Kekchi and Huaxtec words presented in chapter 6 indicated that the Kekchi probably made cornstalk wine aboriginally. It may be possible to find similar correlations in the other languages. There is also much evidence for an aboriginal use of mead (probably without the addition of *balché* bark) among these groups. Flavio Rodas, the well-known translator of the Popol Vuh, told me in Chichicastenango in the spring of 1939 that the Cakchiquel of Sololá still make a beverage by fermenting honey water. They do not use *balché*. Significantly, the mead is made only during Holy Week, which points to a survival of an ancient ritual usage through assimilation into Catholicism. A highly illuminating description of early seventeenth-century usage among the Cakchiquel of Mixco, a town not far from Sacatepéquez, is given by Thomas Gage:

> As for drinking, the *Indians* generally are much given unto it; and drink if they have nothing else, of their poor and simple Chocolatte; without Sugar or many compounds, or of Atolle, until their bellies be ready to burst. But if they can get any drink that will make them mad drunk, they will not give it over as long as a drop is left, or a penny remains in their purse to purchase it. Amongst themselves they use to make such drinks as are in operation far stronger than wine; and these they confection in such great Jarrs as come from *Spain*; wherein they put some little quantity of water, and fill up the Jar with some Melasso's or juice of the Sugar Cane, or some hony for to sweeten it; then for the strengthning of it, they put roots and leaves of Tobacco, with other kinds of roots which grow there, and they know to be strong in operation, nay in some places I have known where they put in a live Toad, and so closed up the Jar for a fortnight, or a months space, till all that they hove [*sic*] put in him, be throughly steeped and the toad consumed, and the drink well strengthened, then they open it, and call their friends to the drinking of it, (which commonly they do in the night time, lest their Priest in the Town should have notice of them in the day) which they never leave off, until they be mad and raging drunk. This drink they call Chicha, which stinketh most filthily, and certainly is the cause of many *Indians* death, especially where they use the toads poyson with it. Once I was informed living in *Mixco*, of a great meeting

that was appointed in an *Indians* house; where I found four Jars of Chicha not yet opened, I caused them to be taken out, and broken in the street before his door, and the filthy Chicha to be poured out, which left such a stinking scent in my nostrils, that with the smell of it, or apprehension of its loathsomness, I fell to vomiting, and continued sick almost a whole week after.[31]

The quotation is sufficiently graphic to need no comment, except for noting that the addition of the toad was by no means trivial but served a definite purpose (see Appendix B).

Wine from jocote was an important beverage in central Guatemala. McBryde collected nine jocote varieties in the neighborhood of Lake Atitlan, of which one of the largest was called "*chicha*" and was used mainly for the purpose of making wine. The variety is ovoid, 1¼ inches long, orange-yellow, rough and thick-skinned, and very acid. It is harvested from September to February. A smaller, yellow variety called "*mico amarillo*" serves the same purpose.[32]

In addition to the above, central Guatemala had two or three other aboriginal beverages. A fiscal report on intoxicating drinks written in 1775 by Josef de Cistue lists beverages made from sugarcane juice in conjunction with "corn, bananas, pineapples, jocotes and other magueys."[33] Sugarcane and bananas (*guineos*) are not aboriginal, although some other kinds of bananas may possibly be. An interesting procedure in connection with beverages of this sort was mentioned to me by Sr. Rodas, a consultant from Chichicastenango, Guatemala, and fully substantiated by other residents of Guatemala. In order to activate such fermenting mixtures, the Cakchiquel of the neighborhood of Sacatepéquez introduce a rag impregnated with the feces of an infant. The procedure is known as "*tanatío*." Such a usage does not seem to have been recorded elsewhere.

Along the south coast of Guatemala, coyol-palm wine is mentioned in many colonial accounts.[34] The Cistue report lists it also for the lowlands of Salvador, Nicaragua, and Nicoya. For the city and province of San Salvador, Cistue mentions:

A variety of chichas are made from a small grain, or bran, jocotes, yams[?] (*Names*), bananas (*Platanos guineos*), pinapples, maguey, *collol*, coco palm (*coco*), corn, and many other plants, that were fermented with cornstalk juice; and, further, from these a strong drink is also made, which all men use, particularly those of color.[35]

Of this list, beverages from "*Platanos guineos*" and "*coco*" are definitely post-Conquest, that from "*Maguei*" almost certainly is, and that from "*Names*" likewise, unless it (really, "*ñames*") was used loosely and referred to the sweet potato (usually called "*camote*" or "*batata*"). Rather than the sweet potato, it was more likely the yam, which had been introduced from Africa in early colonial times; the reference to "men . . . of color" makes one suspect that black slaves were using these ingredients to prepare one of their traditional African intoxicants.

Hog plums were a favorite source of wine in Nicaragua. Oviedo gives the name "*zoxot,*" which was apparently in use among the Nahuatl-speaking Chorotega and shows the typical simplification from the Mexican highland Nahuatl term "*xocotl.*" Oviedo also explains that the *xocot* is similar to the *hobo,* but red instead of yellow and with somewhat more pulp.[36] That description would agree with the identification of *xocot* (jocote) with *Spondias purpurea,* and of *hobo* with *S. mombin,* following the revised classification of Standley (*Trees and Shrubs*). About *xocot* wine, Oviedo remarks: "The wine that is made from this fruit is mediocre . . . but to my way of thinking it [the fruit] is better than the apples of Vizcaya." He also lists fermented drinks of maize and of honey for Nicaragua, as well as other unspecified ones.[37] Cistue lists beverages of maize and coyol as the most common ones of Nicaragua. Of the former he says: "The chichas the Indians sell are made from corn that was cooked, but uncooked when planted, and when it begins to sprout, it is dug up, and made into chicha."[38] This method of actually planting the kernels to make them sprout is rather more primitive than that used in the *tesgüino* region.

In the great interior hill country of Nicaragua and Honduras, the traditional intoxicant appears to be maize beer, in which fermentation is induced by chewing a portion of the mash. The diastatic action of the salivary enzyme, ptyalin, is the stimulant. This trait appears to reach its most northerly limits on the mainland among the Jicaque and Sumu of Honduras, unless by chance some Arawaks took it to the tip of Florida. The trait is mainly South American and Caribbean in distribution. An early eighteenth-century document on the province of Tegucigalpa, after first explaining how the Indians (unspecified) of the area eat human flesh seasoned with chile, states:

> Of the maize they plant, much of it is eaten as green corn. . . . And when it has withered, in a day or two, it is chewed. The masticated corn and tobacco [leaves] that have been soaked in water become what the community drinks. They remain in the infusion for three days, so as to be strong and intoxicating and capable of taking possession of the senses.[39]

It will be remembered that Gage mentions the addition of tobacco also for central Guatemala.[40]

The account of the fourth voyage of Columbus, written by his son Ferdinand, records an encounter with a native canoe off the island of Guanaja, just north of Honduras. Among other things found in the canoe was "a sort of liquor made of Maiz; like the *English* beer."[41]

The coastal people of Honduras and Mosquitia have a great variety of beverages. The so-called Black Carib of the northwest need not be considered, since they did not come into the area until 1796 and since their culture has a strong African admixture.[42] An engineer of many years' residence in Honduras told me in 1939 that he had seen the Paya south of the Patuca River make a beverage of maize and the bark of a certain tree. This bark is used also for cordage and may be similar to the *mecate colorado* of Chiapas. Native names for it are "*guamo*" and "*guama*." For the Sumu and the Miskito, we have an excellent study by Conzemius. Among the Miskito and some of the Sumu, the most important beverage is made with sweet manioc, part of which has been activated by chewing. According to this author, the seventeenth-century accounts do not mention cassava beer, although they list the presence of the plant for food.[43] It is not impossible that the drink may be recent in this area or that the process represents a late transfer from Arawak or Carib culture. Other starchy materials of *Af* regions, such as sweet potatoes and other roots, as well as *pejiballe* fruit, are fermented by the same process. "The fruits of the cashew and other trees, as bananas and plantains, are merely bruised with the addition of water, allowing the juice to take its own time to ferment."[44] The most potent drink is prepared from roasted pineapples.

The main beverages of the Sumu are made from maize. In addition to beer from sprouted corn and from chewed corn, they have another variety that is made from moldy corn:

Dry maize is ground on the metate, wrapped in large leaves after the manner of the "tamales" of the Ladinos, and thus cooked in boiling water. It is then kept for weeks or months over the smoke of the fire, whereby it becomes covered with a grayish mold, which accounts for its name (*puput*, "gray"). A few days previous to the celebration of the feast the mass is taken out of the leaves, crumbled, and cooked with a small quantity of water; it is then poured in a hole made in the ground over which a provisional shed has been erected. A thick layer of Bijagua leaves or of balsa bark prevents the beverage from coming in contact with the ground. In two or three days fermentation will be completed and then the drink is ready for the palate. Before being served this potent liquor is strained and mixed with water.[45]

Conzemius adds that a similar method of preparing corn beer has been observed in the Guianas, and a similar one will be mentioned in the next paragraph for the Bribri of Costa Rica. Other beverages listed for the people of the

Mosquito Coast include wines from the stems of coyol and corozo palms, and some unverified beverages from annatto seeds and from the fruit pulp of the wild cacao.[46] According to Martínez Landero, the Sumu consider intoxicating drinks as tonics for the system. As a result, not only the adults but also the children consume quantities of alcoholic beverages. Landero was for a time in charge of an elementary school among the Sumu, and he records that he always had one or two children in attendance who were under the influence of alcohol.[47]

Among the Bribri Indians of the Caribbean coast of Costa Rica, Pittier found three kinds of corn chicha. The first is made by grinding maize kernels with an equal proportion of desiccated bananas. The meal is boiled in water. A small proportion of the maize is chewed and the impregnated material added to the fermenting mixture. In from twelve to twenty-four hours, the chicha is ready to drink. The second variety is made only from maize, which is ground, made into tortillas, and toasted over the fire. When the tortillas are cool, they are mashed up in water, with some of them chewed and added to the mixture. The fermentation is allowed to proceed for eight days, and produces a particularly nauseous beverage. The third type is made from sprouted maize, which is ground with ripe bananas and then baked in the fire in the form of small cakes. These are then kept until they are thoroughly decomposed by mildew, at which time they are ground and mixed with an appropriate amount of the second chicha listed above. The resultant fermentation gives an extremely intoxicating drink. In addition to these corn beers the Bribri also use chichas of *pejiballe* and of manioc.[48]

The account of Ferdinand Columbus for Veragua, already cited in connection with palm wine, mentions, in addition to coyol, beverages from maize, pineapples, and mameys (see note 15, this chapter). A letter written in 1575 by Pedro Godinez Osorio referring to Guaymí in northwestern Panama relates:

The Indians know maize as a sustenance and palms are an even more principal sustenance. The fruits of the palms are called "*pejibaes*," and "*yuca*," and "*Piñas*." And from these, they make a certain drink they call "*masamorra*," which is nourishing and also intoxicating.[49]

Oviedo describes in detail the preparation of maize beer in Panama. According to his statement, the kernels are allowed to sprout and are then boiled in water to which certain herbs are added. The mixture is boiled for a considerable length of time, after which the vessel is removed from the fire and the contents are allowed to cool. The sediment is not strained out. On the third and fourth days, the beverage is in its best state for drinking. (It is again puzzling that he does not say anything regarding the addition of saliva to the fermenting mixture.) In addition,

Oviedo mentions pineapple wine for eastern Panama and also for the north coast of South America, known in his day as Tierra Firme.[50]

A posthumous publication of Nordenskiöld has shown that the most important alcoholic beverage of the Cuna Indians in easternmost Panama is a wine made from plantains and bananas.[51] Any interpretation thereof hinges on an ultimate determination of the aboriginal status of the banana in the New World.

APPENDIX A

Checklist of Intoxicating Beverages

I. Northwest Cactus Region

	Sahuaro (Mead)	Pitahaya	Mescal	Tuna	*Tesgüino*	Mesquite	Elderberry
Maricopa	X						
Pima	X	?	X	X	X	X	X
Papago	X	X	X			X	
Ópata		X	X	X	X	X	
Cahita		X	X	X	X	X	
Guasave		X		X		X	

II. *Tesgüino* Region

	Tesgüino	Mescal	Cornstalk	Sotol	Guayaba
Tarahumar	X	X	X	?	
Tepehuán	X	X	?	X	
Tubar	X	?			
Varohío	?	X			
Acaxee	?	?			
Xixime	?	?			
Huichol	X	X	?	X	?

III. Tuna and Mesquite Region

	Tuna	Mesquite	Mescal
Zacatec	X	X	X
Guachichil	X	X	X
Lagunero		X	?
Chichimeca	X	X	X
Pame	X	X	X

IV. Pulque Region

	Pulque	Hog Plum (*Spondias*)	Honey	Mescal	Pine-apple	Palm Sap	Corn-stalk	*Tesgüino*	Tuna	Guana-bana
Nahua (incl. Nahuatl)	X						X		X	
Otomí (Highland)							X	?		
Otomí (Puebla)	X						X			
Mazahua	X						X	X		
Tarasca	X	X	X	X			X	?		
Cazcan	X			X				X	X	
Huaxtec	X	X		?			X			
Cuicatec	X	X				X				X
Mixtec	X			X	X					
Zapotec	X			X						
Mixe	?									

V. Mescal and Jocote Region

	Mescal	Jocote	Jocuistle	(Ampelocissus acapulcensis) "Uva"
Tahue	X	X		
Cora	X	?	X	
Totorame	X	?		
Otomí (Jalisco)	X	X		
Otomí (Western Jalisco)	X	X		
Nahua (Colima, southern Michoacán)	X	X		?
Nahua (Western Guerrero)	?	?		

A. West of the Maya-Quiché

	Honey	Corn-stalk	Pine-apple	Banana	Hog Plum	Mescal	Mamey	Sarsa-parilla	Palm Sap	Capulín	Maize & Mecate Beer
Tlapanec	X	?									
Tepuztec or (Tepetixtec)		X	X	X	X	X					
Matzatec			X								
Chinantec			X		X		X				
Totonac		X	X					X		X	
Nahua (southern Veracruz & Chiapas)	?										
Tzotzil									X		X

B. *Balché* Region

	Honey & *Balché*	Palm Sap	Pineapple	Piñuela	Chicozapote
Maya	X				
Lacandón	X	X	X	X	X

Auxiliary Herbs

Group	Beverage	Herb Added	Taxonomic Name of Herb
White Mountain Apache	*tesgüino*	loco weed (jimson weed)	*Datura meteloides*
San Carlos Apache	*tesgüino*	mesquite bark	*Prosopis chilensis*
White Mountain Apache San Carlos Apache Chiricahua Apache Mescalero Apache	*tesgüino*	unidentified roots	
Tarahumar	*tesgüino*	brome grass	*Bromus* sp.
		lichen	*Usnea* sp.
		"mosslike plants"	*Selaginella inspida*ta *Chimaphila lacudata* *Stevia* sp.
		sedge	*Fimbristylis* sp.
		copalquín	*Coutarea pterosperma*
	mescal wine	*gotóko*	(Leguminosae)
		papache	*Randia echinocarpa*
	cornstalk wine	*gotóko*	(Leguminosae)
Varohío	mescal wine	*nawo*	*Phaseolus caracalla*
Mazahua	*sendechó* (*tesgüino*)	teposan chile	*Buddleia americana* *Capsicum annuum*
Totonac	cornstalk wine	*limacatlín* (*timbre*)	*Calliandra laxa*
Nahua	pulque	*ocpatli*	?
Zapotec		*quauhpatli*	*Acacia angustissima*
Mixtec Cuicatec		*árbol del Perú* (seed; bark)	*Schinus molle*

Otomí	pulque	peyote	*Lophophora williamsii*
Chinantec	pineapple wine	*tepesimatl*	?
	jocote wine		?
	mamey wine		
Maya	*balché*	*balché*	*Lonchocarpus longistylus*
		agave root	*Agave* sp.
Tzotzil	corn or maize chicha	*mecate colorado*	?
Cakchiquel	mead	tobacco	*Nicotiana* sp.
Paya	corn chicha	*guamo*; *guama*	?
Sumu	corn chicha	tobacco	*Nicotiana* sp.

To this list should be added a toad as an ingredient in wine made from honey as reported by Gage for the Cakchiquel.[1] The toad has properties similar to those of some herbs that are used to enhance alcoholic beverages, as is described below.

In the main, the various herbs in the above table are put into the fermenting mixtures for specific purposes, though these need not be consciously expressed or even precisely recognized. We may safety infer that a number of different purposes are involved in this lengthy though incomplete list. It is entirely unwarranted to impose unfounded superstition on a primitive people in the concoction of their recipes. A much safer attitude is that a long empirical experimental procedure has gone before and that the ingredients that to us are obscure or of questionable utility have proven their worth by trial and error.

These herbs may have a number of functions that are not readily evident. They may, for example, (1) be a means by which the proper organisms for fermentation are introduced into the mixture; (2) serve as a source of bios factors for the fermentation organisms; (3) contain, in the case of *tesgüino*, activators for the fermentation of maltose sugars; and (4) contain constituents that affect differentially the growth of micro-organisms in the fermenting mixture.[2]

In addition to affecting the microflora of the beverages, some of these herbs have other qualities. Thus, there is a group of herbs that are usually taken separately rather than in alcoholic beverages. They are employed because of the effects on the consumer of the alkaloids they contain. Peyote, datura, and tobacco at once stand out as members of this group. There is a second category having strong and unique flavors, whose main function appears to be to add a distinctive aroma and taste to the beverage. Chile in *sendechó* and *Schinus* in pulque seem to belong here. Some of the Tarahumar and Apache herbs may also be similarly utilized.

The final group is the most interesting of all. It includes plants that may contain in their bark or root certain saponins that act as cardiac poisons. Such heart poisons have for the most part a cyclopentenophenanthrene nucleus in their molecules, and hence are closely related to the digitalis complex, which exhibits a similar structure, as well as to many tropical arrow poisons and fish poisons.[3]

The various barks and roots, to which *ocpatli, quauhpatli, limacatlín, tepesimatl, mecate colorado,* and *balché* belong, and perhaps *gotóko* and mesquite likewise, not to mention the many unrecorded plants utilized in this area and elsewhere, often contain tannin as part of their chemical composition. The percentage of tannin is so great in some cases that the plants are commonly used in native tanning practices. However, we may be quite certain that the roots and barks just listed are not added to beverages because of their tannin content. The tannin may result in a slightly better flavor and a clearer liquid, but such considerations are set aside. Intoxicating power is the prime consideration. The chances are that tannin is incidental compared to the desired constituent, the heart stimulant. No conclusive evidence of the presence of these cardiac glycosides has yet been obtained since the requisite physiological tests have not been given. However, saponin has been demonstrated in at least two of the specimens, *limacatlín* and *mecate colorado*; a water solution of each bark quickly hemolyzed red blood corpuscles that had been washed and centrifuged.[4] *Mecate colorado* has not been identified botanically, but *limacatlín* is a *Calliandra* (*C. laxa*, according to Professor Herbert Louis Mason, University of California, Berkeley). Standley mentions that *Calliandra anomala* and *C. houstoniana* are used as auxiliary roots in fermented drinks, and relates that the latter "is said to contain an alkaloid which produces death by systolic arrest of the heart."[5] More likely the substance is not an alkaloid but rather a saponin heart poison. This point needs to be checked in the laboratory.

Although definite information is lacking, it is dangerous to generalize, but what evidence there is leads one to suspect that heart poisons are the main physiologically active substances introduced into fermenting mixture through the addition of pulque roots and related products. According to Fieser, these heart poisons, like digitalis extract, act as excitants in small quantities and raise the pulse rate. Artificially heightened stimulation in ritual drunkenness, leading to extreme exhaustion when the frenzy is over, must intensify the ceremonial significance of the act.[6]

The hypothesis that these herbs are mainly heart stimulants receives considerable support from another quarter. According to Fieser, only two classes of specific heart poisons occur in nature. The one kind is the particular category of plant saponins with cyclopentenophenanthrene nuclei described above. The other kind occurs in the skin of the toad (*Bufo* spp.). Toad poisons are not saponins, but are structurally related to cardiac poisons of vegetable origin and have similar physiological properties.[7]

In the case of adding a toad to a fermented drink, as described in detail by Gage for the Cakchiquel, the problem of what is the desired constituent becomes rather simple: (1) No tannin is introduced into the beverage; (2) the addition of fermentation organisms, if needed, could certainly be accomplished in other ways than by adding a live toad; and (3) the flavor of the beverage with the toad is far less desirable than the flavor without the toad—the final result probably "stinketh most filthily" even to the drinker. Even rational human beings will not ordinarily take to something with a repulsive stench unless some craving is thereby satisfied. Furthermore, in consuming decayed flesh an individual is taking a great risk of poisoning, since the ptomaines are common decomposition products of protein putrefaction, especially at somewhat elevated temperatures. Apparently the Cakchiquel who made mead with a toad often suffered as a consequence, for, as Gage remarks: "This drink . . . is the cause of many *Indians* death, especially where they put the toads poyson with it."[8] These deaths may occasionally result from ptomaine poisoning, but they may also result from an overdose of the cardiac stimulant, resulting in systolic arrest of the heart.

The reason for putting in the toad must be some quality inherent in the toad itself, a quality powerful and desirable enough to overcome a natural revulsion against the effluvium of decayed meat. There can be only one explanation: the heart stimulant. As suggested before, small quantities of these substances increase the pulse rate and apparently heighten the general state of excitement, thus aiding in the realization of a condition that is ritualistically desirable. Gage records that the Indians who drank this concoction became "mad and raging drunk."[9]

The clear-cut case of the toad lends confirmation to the case regarding the function of pulque roots and related substances and suggests by analogy the explanations of associated phenomena. The deaths from *ocpatli* in the area around Puebla, as cited in a late seventeenth-century document discussed in chapter 7, may easily have been caused by heart failure resulting from an excessive dose of the pulque root.

Classification of Intoxicating Beverages

A. Maize Drinks (*Zea mays*)
  1. Sprouted
    a. *Tesgüino*
      i. Without peyote - Huichol, etc.
      ii. With peyote - Tarahumara
    b. *Sendechó*
      i. Only of maize
      ii. Chile, or pulque or *tepozán* leaves, or aguardiente added
  2. Chewed — Chicha
      i. Only of maize
      ii. Tobacco juice, banana, or yuca (*Manihot* spp.) added
B. Cut Bud-Tip Drinks
  1. *Agave* — Pulque (*octli* - Nahuatl)
      i. Pure (various agaves to be differentiated)
      ii. Pirul seeds (*Schinus molle*), or pulque root, or *timbre*, or *panela* added
  2. *Cocos*, *Attalea*, etc.
    a. *Tuba*
    b. *Taberna* (from coyol [*Acrocomia mexicana*])
    c. Other palm wines (*guapilla* palm - Tehuantepac?)
C. Baked Plant-Heart Drinks
  1. *Agave*
    a. Distilled - mescal, *bacanora*, *tusca* (Tuxcacuesco and Tuxpan, Jalisco), *comiteco*, tequila, *mescal de olla*
    b. Not distilled - "*tuba*" (Bolaños)
  2 *Dasylirion* (sotol)
    a. Distilled — *tuchi*
    b. Not distilled — "*tuba*" (Guadalupe Ocotán)
D. Cactus Fruit Drinks — saguaro pitahaya, etc. (Colonche, Colorado, Tes, etc.)

E. Other Fruit Drinks
    1. Pineapple (*tepache*, with and without *panela*)
    2. Piñuela (*Bromelia* spp.)
    3. Capulín (*Prunus* spp.)
        i. Fleshy part
        ii. Seeds
    4. *Nanche* (*Byrsonima crassifolia*)
    5. *Jocuistle* (*Bromelia* spp.)
    6. *Uva címarron* (*Vitis* spp.)
    7. Guanabana (*Annona* sp.)
F. Flower Drinks — *xtabentún*?
G. Honey Drinks (mead)
    1. Only honey
    2. With *balché* (*Lonchocarpus longistylus*)
H. Root Drinks
    1. *Yuca* (*Manihot* spp.) — chewed
    2. Sarsaparilla (*Smilax* spp.)?
I. Grass-Stalk Drinks
    1. Cornstalks
        a. Not distilled?
        b. Distilled? — refined aguardiente, "pulque"
J. Distilled Pulque?
K. Seeds of Balsam del Peru?
L. Mesquite?
M. Animal Drinks
    1. Fermented honey ants?
    2. "Alcoholic" worms?

Spelling of Latin botanical names for plants provided by James A. Bauml.

Classification is by Henry J. Bruman, Field Notebook III, Mexico, May 1939. Fowler Museum of Cultural History, UCLA.

Notes

1. V. Havard, *Drink Plants of the North American Indians*, Torrey Botanical Club Bulletin 23 (1896): 37–38.

Ethnologists give another explanation. An absolutely necessary condition for alcoholic fermentation to occur is the presence of suitable microorganisms. The native distribution of such organisms has never been worked out in detail, but it is by no means so extensive as has been believed. Even in the late nineteenth century there were viticultural areas in California so deficient in suitable microflora that fermentation of grape juice in those areas did not occur. It is possible, therefore, that a fermentable liquid could have been exposed by the eastern Indians with no other results than eventual molding and putrefaction. I am indebted to Professor M. A. Joslyn of the Department of Fruit Products, College of Agriculture, University of California, Berkeley, for this information.

2. E. J. Payne, *History of the New World Called America*, vol. 1 (Oxford, 1892), 406.

3. Fages's report reads: "In the canyons of the Santa Clara, there are many willows (*Sauces*), from the fruit of which, when ripe, the Indians know how to make a certain wine that does not taste bad" (Report to Bucareli of November 14, 1775, Biblioteca Nacional de México, legato 53, no. 37 [Mexico City]). See chapter 2, note 22, for additional information on this document.

H. I. Priestley (*A Historical, Political, and Natural Description of California by Pedro Fages, Soldier of Spain* [Berkeley, 1937], 22) translates *Sauces* quite correctly as willows. But the "fruit" of the willow seems hardly likely material for the manufacture of wine. Most likely we are dealing here with a slip of the pen by the contemporary copyist, or perhaps by Fages himself, in writing *Sauces* instead of *Saucos*. *Saucos* (correctly *Saúcos*, but accents are generally omitted in this document) are elderberries, which are plentiful in the canyons of southern California. Their aboriginal use for wine is well established elsewhere, in particular among the Pima Alto of Sonora.

4. F. W. Waugh, *Iroquois Foods and Food Preparation*, Canada Department of Mines, Geological Survey Memoir no. 86 (Ottawa, 1916), 140–41, 146.

5. Ibid., 54–57.

6. W. Hough, *The Hopi Indians* (Cedar Rapids, Iowa, 1915), 64; M. C. Stevenson, *Ethnology of the Zuñi Indians*, Smithsonian Institution, Bureau of American Ethnology 30th Annual Report (Washington, D.C. 1915), 68, 71.

7. Stevenson, *Zuñi Indians*, 76. *Tesgüino* is a beer made by the fermentation of malted (sprouted) corn that has been ground, mixed with water, and boiled for many hours. For a full discussion of this drink, see chapter 4.

8. F. H. Cushing, *Zuñi Breadstuff*, Indian Notes and Monographs, vol. 8 (New York, 1920), 635.

"The juice which exuded from the plants from which the hearts had been cut was collected in large vessels, allowed to ferment, and thus formed, when imbibed in large quantities, a fiercely intoxicating drink." The procedure mentioned in this statement is most unlikely, since the varieties of mescal agave that grow in the Southwest do not exude juice after the hearts are removed. In fact, all that is left of the plant is a bit of root and the slender leaves. The statement probably should be interpreted as a dim memory of the typical fermentation of the baked agave heart.

9. E. F. Castetter, W. H. Bell, and A. R. Grove, *The Early Utilization and the Distribution of Agave in the American Southwest*, University of New Mexico Bulletin no. 335 (Albuquerque, 1938), 27–38, 60, 62.

The Apache techniques entail certain modifications of the usual pattern. For example, the Mescalero and Chiricahua fermented roasted mescal in pouches of animal hide buried in the ground for two days. The Apache of the Fort Apache region of Arizona allowed the pit baking to continue for fifteen days before removing the mescal heads and fermenting them. The White Mountain Apache apparently fermented only the flower stalk. Cremony is cited as recording for several Apache groups the boiling down of mescal wine "to produce a strong intoxicating beverage." If carried on after fermentation, as the statement implies, this procedure would serve to reduce rather than to increase the alcoholic strength of the beverage. It may be, of course, that certain alkaloid-bearing roots were boiled in the wine to increase the intoxicating power (see note 12, below).

10. A. Hrdlička, "Method of Preparing Texvino among the White River Apaches," *American Anthropologist*, n.s., 6 (1904): 190–91; A. Hrdlička, *Physiological and Medical Observations among the Indians of Southwestern United States and Northern Mexico*, Smithsonian Institution, Bureau of American Ethnology Bulletin no. 34 (Washington, D.C., 1908), 22–29.

The Apache call *tesgüino* "*tulipi*," which means "yellow water." The White River Apache learned how to brew it after 1850 from the Chiricahua, who in turn were said to have learned it in Mexico. It is because of this late learning process that the Apache are not considered in the scheme of aboriginal drink regions as presented here. The procedure that Hrdlička describes for the manufacture of *tulipi* by the White River Apache is similar to the usual recipe in vogue in the *tesgüino* area, but entails two noteworthy differences. After the first boiling, "*tulipi* medicine" is added, which in the case of the White River Apache consists of the root of the jimson weed (*Datura meteloides*), a powerful drug. The other point of interest is the adding of some coarsely ground wheat to the must before fermenting. This step would suggest that the Chiricahua learned *tesgüino* brewing from the Pima, since, through Jesuit influence, wheat came to be more important in the diet of the Pima than maize, and even exerted an influence on ritual foods and drinks. The step suggests further that the trait goes back ultimately to the Tarahumar, who invariably add at this stage the ground seeds of a native grass (*Bromus* sp.) that looks very much like wild oats. It is doubtful whether the addition of these cereal grains is technologically necessary. It may be merely a ritualistic adjunct.

Hrdlička made a special effort to ascertain the "medicines" added by the San Carlos Apache to the *tesgüino* and the reasons for it. He found eight kinds of roots in use for which he lists the native names, although only four of these have been toxonomically identified: *Lotus wrightii, Cassia couesii, Canotia holocantha,* and *Perezi wrightii.* Most of these were added for the expressed purpose of making the drink more intoxicating. He also found that the inner bark of the mesquite was occasionally added in order to make the drink taste sweeter. It seems likely that the adding of herbs was part of the *tesgüino* complex that spread northward along the Sierra.

11. Hrdlička, *Physiological and Medical Observations,* 28. Here again a change in the process is apparent. Instead of fermenting the whole fruit, including in the must pulp and seeds, which are later removed, the fruit is "put into large jars. The pressure of the soft fruit causes an abundant supply of the juices to trickle out; this is poured off and allowed to ferment."

12. The species of pine is not given. Ibid., 22, 27.

13. A similar case may be the fermented drink from the bananalike fruit of various species of yucca, mentioned by Havard (*Drink Plants,* 37) for the Chihuahua (*sic*) Indians. It is hard to know what to do with this undocumented, uncorroborated reference. Perhaps Havard meant Chiricahua, as W. La Barre assumes ("Native American Beers," *American Anthropologist,* n.s., 40 [1938]: 231).

14. C. O. Sauer, "The Distribution of Aboriginal Tribes and Languages in North-Western Mexico," *Ibero-Americana* 5 (1934): 44.

15. W J McGee, *The Seri Indians,* Smithsonian Institution, Bureau of American Ethnology 17th Annual Report (Washington, D.C., 1898); see also A. L. Kroeber, *The Seri,* Southwest Museum Papers no. 6 (Los Angeles, 1931).

16. Memorias para la historia de Sinaloa, *Carta anua* (1593), MS 227, Mex., p. 86, University of California, Berkeley, Bancroft Library.

17. The possibility that the Seri may have come by boat from Baja California seems more unlikely, especially since the Baja California Yumans had no pottery.

18. See especially J. Baegert, *Nachrichten von der Amerikanishen Halbinsel Californien* (Mannheim, 1772).

19. A. Woodward, "The 'Honey' of the Early California Indians: A Strange Ethnological Error," *The Masterkey* 12 (1938): 175–80.

20. Biblioteca Nacional de México, "*Costumbres de los Indios Apaches (Lipanes),*" 4 ff, legajo 99, no. 66 [filing system prior to 1939] (Mexico City); "*Carta escrita de Nachitos p^r el Cavallero Macartij ad^n Angel Marios y Navarrete en 17 de 9bre de 1763,*" lf.–v. (Mexico City): "They do not become intoxicated and they abhore all strong drink. They do not use intoxicating herbs."

21. F. C. Chabot, *Excerpts from the Memorias for the History of the Province of Texas* (Morfi, 1932), xiv, n. 18. From the citation it is not clear whether 1709 or 1716 is the date.

22. W. La Barre, *The Peyote Cult,* Yale University Publications in Anthropology no. 19 (New Haven, Connecticut, 1938), 23.

23. Ibid., 121.

24. Havard, *Drink Plants,* 40–42. See also F. W. Hodge, ed., *Handbook of American Indians North of Mexico* (Washington, D.C., 1907–1910) (under "Black drink") and La Barre (*Peyote Cult,* 133) for a list of tribes using the beverage. Cabeza de Vaca observed the use of

this brew, and Oviedo mentions it in his account, without, however, referring to it by name (*In* G. F. de Oviedo, *Historia general y natural* . . . , vol. 3 [Madrid, 1852], 595).

25. Havard, *Drink Plants*, 40.

26. It may also contain a substance with sudorific and diuretic properties (ibid., 91).

27. E. M. Hale quoted by Havard (ibid., 41). Havard (ibid., 41) mentions the addition of *Eryngium aquaticum* ("button snakeroot"), *Iris versicolor*, and *Lobelia inflata* to provide a strong emetic effect. It is possible that these herbs, or others that were added, may contain alkaloids that resulted in a certain degree of temporary psychic derangement.

CHAPTER 2

1. In some areas, sotol (*Dasylirion* sp.) tended to replace or supplement agave; in others, mesquite or the various cactus fruits were locally more important. But none of these had such consistent importance, coupled with wide distribution, as mescal. The great age of sotol baking in the Big Bend area of Texas is corroborated by the finding of sotol pits in a Basket Maker horizon in Brewster County. Recognizable fragments of sotol fiber were recovered (R. M. Zingg, *A Reconstruction of Uto-Aztecan History*, University of Denver Contributions to Ethnography no. 2 [New York, 1939]).

2. Cf. map in R. Beals, "The Comparative Ethnology of Northern Mexico before 1750," *Ibero-Americana* 2 (1932): 159.

3. Even in the recent past, people have occasionally found it useful for this purpose. During a food shortage in the middle of the nineteenth century the whole town of Presidio del Norte (El Paso) managed to get along for six months on baked mescal (Bartlett quoted in Hodge, *Handbook*, vol. 1 [Washington, D.C., 1907], 846).

Portions of baked mescal hearts are sometimes sold as a cheap sweetstuff to the urbanized lower stratum of Mexico City, as I observed in 1939 in the Mercado de la Merced.

4. Recorded for the Chichimeca by Juan de Cárdenas, *Problemas y secretos maravillosos de las Indias* (Mexico, lst ed. 1591; 2d ed. 1913). See chapter 5.

5. V. Santa Maria, *Relación histórica de la Colonia del Nuevo Santander, México*, Archivo General Publicación no. 15 (1930), 406.

6. Castetter, Bell, and Grove, *Early Utilization*, 51.

7. Biblioteca Nacional de México, *Relación geográfica* for the Cora Mission, Jesús María y José, 1777, MS 15-3-76.

8. C. Lumholtz, *Unknown Mexico: A Record of Five Years' Exploration*, vol. 1 (New York, 1902) 402, 478.

9. The mescal agave will flower only once in its lifetime—when from eight to fourteen years old—and then generally in early summer after the first rains. Thus, the supply of *quiotes* or flower shoots will undergo strong seasonal fluctuations. The crowns, on the other hand, can be used at any time after the plant has reached a certain degree of maturity.

10. W. Trelease, "Agave," *in* P. C. Standley, *Trees and Shrubs of Mexico*, Contributions from the U.S. National Herbarium no. 23, 5 parts (Washington, D.C., 1920–1926), 107–42; A. Berger, *Die Agaven* (Jena, 1915).

11. Berger, *Agaven*, 8–9.

12. W. Trelease, *Agave in the West Indies*, Memoirs of the National Academy of Sciences no. 11 (1913).

13. The name "Mexico" seems to be ultimately derivable from "*metl.*" M. Orozco y Berra (*Historia antigua de la conquista de México*, vol. 1 [Mexico, 1880], 457–60) has summarized

the evidence. "Mexico" means "the place of *Mexitli*." *Mexitli* is variously identified as one of the chiefs who led the Aztec tribe to the site of Tenochtitlan and as a pseudonym of the war god Huitzilopochtli. At any rate, his hieroglyphic symbol contains the elements of a maguey plant (*metl*) and the "navel" (*xictli*) of the maguey (the hole in which the aguamiel for pulque is collected).

14. C. A. Robelo, *Diccionario de Aztequismos* (Cuernavaca, 1904), 598.

15. In fact, Prieto (*Historia, geografía y estadística del Estado de Tamaulipas* [Mexico, 1873], 252–53) specifically mentions *flor de la pitahaya* as a common food of the Tamaulipeca, and the word "pitahaya" is always restricted to mean fiber agaves.

16. R. E. Crist, "Some Geographic Aspects of the Manufacture of Mezcal," *Scientific Monthly* 50 (March, 1940): 324–36.

17. For a good summary of the evidence as well as for a general study of the distribution and utilization of mescal in the Southwest and adjacent areas, see Castetter, Bell, and Grove, *Early Utilization of Agave.*

18. In spite of the fact that agave roasting pits have not been found archaeologically in the southern part of the peninsula, the evidence in favor of the aboriginal utilization of mescal for food is conclusive. In the report of Jaime Bravo ("*Razon de la entrada al Puerto de la Paz, Conquista de la Nación Guaycura, y fundación de la Misión de Nuestra Señora del Pilar en California, año de 1720*," MS, Biblioteca Nacional de México, legajo 53, no. 19° [Mexico City]), deer, manioc, mescal, and fish are mentioned among the foods of the Guaicuru, south of the Bahia de la Paz. Similarly, Baegert (*Amerikanischen Halbinsel Californien*), for the area about Lat. 25°, describes the process of mescal roasting in shallow, apparently impermanent pits.

19. Cushing, *Zuñi Breadstuff*, 635. See chapter 1.

20. For the Big Bend country, the distribution of archaeologic baking pits is given by Castetter, Bell, and Grove (*Early Utilization of Agave*, 37), and by E. B. Sayles (*An Archaeologic Survey of Texas*, Medallion Papers no. 17 [Gila Pueblo, Globe, Arizona, 1935], 134. The testimony of Alonso de León (*in* G. García and C. Pereyra, *Doc. inéd. ó muy raros hist. Méj.*, vol. 25, 37–38) records the baking of mescal among the Coahuilteca of Nuevo Leon, in the neighborhood of Cerralvo. The Tamaulipeca to the southeast did not bake mescal hearts (see also Santa Maria, *Relación histórica*, 406; and note 15, above).

21. The Huaxteca itself presents a troublesome borderline case. True mescal species may have reached down to the coastal plain, just as certain inferior pulque agaves did. Botanically the region is very imperfectly known. A native term for mescal is given in the Huaxtec word list of Tapia Zenteno (see chapter 7, n. 6), but the word may come from the higher western portion known as the Huaxteca Potosina.

22. There still remains to be explained a curious statement made by Pedro Fages in his report to Bucareli of November, 1775. The copy examined was dated November 14, 1775, and is located in the Biblioteca Nacional de México, legajo 53, no. 37. Priestley has published a translation of a copy dated November 20, 1775, located apparently in the Museo Nacional de México (Priestley, *Description by Pedro Fages*). Referring to the area around San Luis Obispo, California, Fages says: "There is much maguey of the kind the Mexicans call mescalli." He describes the process of mescal baking in considerable detail, and mentions that a good wine can be made from the roasted mescal buds, though he seems to imply that such a wine was not made by the California Indians. The odd thing about the story is that San Luis Obispo lies far beyond the natural range of mescal. Such plants do not grow wild within a radius of more than 200 miles. Apparently Fages, who was otherwise a trustworthy observer, mistook

the plentiful wild yuccas for agaves, and the baking of yucca shoots for the preparation of mescal.

23. The description is a composite summary that represents average conditions over most of the mescal area. For specific procedures, see Hodge, *Handbook*, vol. 1, 845–46; L. Spier, *Yuman Tribes of the Gila River* (Chicago, 1933), 55; L. Spier, *Havasupai Ethnography* (New York, 1928), 106; A. L. Kroeber, *Walapai Ethnography*, American Anthropological Association Memoir no. 42, 49 (Menasha, Wisconsin, 1935); W. C. Bennett and R. M. Zingg, *The Tarahumara: An Indian tribe of Northern Mexico* (Chicago, 1935), 148.

24. L. Pérez, *Estudio sobre el maguey llamado mezcal en el Estado de Jalisco* (Guadalajara, 1887), 18, 24; also L. Diguet, "*Etude sur le Maguey de Tequila*," *Revue de Cultures Coloniales*, vol. 10 (1902): 324.

25. Pérez, *Estudio sobre el maguey*, 24. However, Hartwich (*Die menschlichen Genussmittel . . .* [Leipzig, 1911], 645) makes an undocumented statement to the effect that the roasted heads contain 9.2 percent sucrose and 24.8 percent fructose.

26. T. Motolinía (de Benavente), *Historia de los indios de la Nueva España*, D. Sánchez García edition (Barcelona, 1914), 251.

27. Lumholtz, *Unknown Mexico*, vol. 1, 256; Bennett and Zingg, *Tarahumara*, 149.

28. Bennett and Zingg, *Tarahumara*, 149.

29. Regarding the accessory plants, see chapter 4 and Appendix B.

30. H. S. Gentry, *The Warihio Indians of Sonora-Chihuahua: An ethnographic survey*, Smithsonian Institution, Bureau of American Ethnology Anthropological Paper no. 65 (Washington, D.C., 1963). The aboriginal culture of these people has undergone great changes. Also see Sauer, "Aboriginal Tribes and Languages," 36.

31. Could this be the same as the Tarahumar *gotóko*?

32. Rémi Siméon, *Dictionnaire de la langue Nahuatl* (Paris, 1885). The native word for yucca, *isote*, comes from a similar form, *icçotl*, which is given as *palmier des montagnes*. A related word is *soyate*, Nahuatl *çoyatl*, translated as *palmier, palme*. The last named is widely applied along the west coast to certain palms from which fiber for "straw" hats is obtained. In different areas of Mexico, these three native terms have been applied to many different plants, even to plants of different genera (see M. Martínez, *Catálogo de nombres vulgares y científicos de plantas mexicanas* [Mexico, 1937]). The syllable *co* in a plant name evidently refers to a palmlike habit, even if the resemblance is remote. It is obvious, for example, that no argument can be based on an attempt to prove that "coco" is a native American word and that hence the coconut is a native American plant.

33. Standley (*Trees and Shrubs*) lists sixteen for Mexico.

34. Martínez (*Catálogo*, 441) records this usage in the state of San Luis Potosí.

35. S. B. Buckley (*Second Annual Report of the Geological and Agricultural Survey of Texas* [Houston, 1876], 65) was told by some Mexicans that it was roasted and eaten for food.

36. Bennett and Zingg, *Tarahumara*, 165.

37. A. Hrdlička, "The Region of the Ancient 'Chichimecs,' with Notes on the Tepecano and the Ruin of La Quemada, Mexico," *American Anthropologist*, n.s., 5 (1903): 410.

38. R. F. Hare, S. R. Mitchell, and A. P. Bjerregaard (*Denatured Alcohol from Tunas and Other Sources*, New Mexico Agricultural Experiment Station, Bulletin no. 72 [Albuquerque, August 1909], 29) give the following percentage composition: Water, 70.00; protein, 1.22; fat, 0.68; carbohydrates (nitrogen-free extract), 17.33; ash, 1.96; fiber, 8.81; starch, none; sugar, 4.53.

H. L. Shantz and R. Zon ("Natural Vegetation," in *Atlas of American Agriculture* [(Washington, D.C., 1924], 25) make the following statement regarding *Dasylirion texanum* in the Big Bend country: "During periods of drought the sotol is chopped open and cattle subsist on the thickened bases of the leaves, which are relatively high in sugar content and are considered exceptionally good emergency feed."

39. M. Martínez (*Plantas utiles de México*, 2d ed. [Mexico, 1936], 371–72) has a picture of *Dasylirion durangense* heads ready for baking and a wooden fermenting vat from somewhere in Durango.

CHAPTER 3

1. The information regarding the distribution and aboriginal utilization of sahuaro and related forms in this area is summarized by E. F. Castetter and W. H. Bell, *The Aboriginal Utilization of the Tall Cacti in the American Southwest*, University of New Mexico Bulletin no. 307 (Albuquerque, 1937).

2. Ibid., 8. The information is derived mainly from Forrest Shreve.

3. Ibid., 9.

4. The Western Apache make sahuaro wine today, but it seems likely that they learned that art relatively recently, as is the case also with their fermented maize beverage, as recorded by Hrdlička ("Methods of Preparing Texvino," 190–91). Hrdlička likewise mentions sahuaro wine, but the Ópata merely graze the edge of the sahuaro country along their extreme western margin, and the author (Juan Nentvig?) of the *Rudo ensayo* (trans. by Eusebio Guitéras [1951], 49-54) gives a strong impression that the sahuaro was not used by them.

The Yuma, oddly enough, never took to sahuaro wine, in spite of the fact that their close relatives on the Gila River, the Maricopa, made much of it. The only alcoholic beverages recorded for the Yuma would appear to be a late post-Conquest aberration of *tesgüino*. It is a brew made by the fermentation of roasted wheat grains, and is called "*pissioina*" (Hrdlička, *Physiological and Medical Observations*, 28).

5. Lumholtz, *New Trails in Mexico* (New York, 1912), 47; F. Russell, *The Pima Indians*, Smithsonian Institution, Bureau of American Ethnology 26th Annual Report (Washington, D.C., 1808), 71.

6. The precise details for the Papago are given by Castetter and Bell (*Aboriginal Utilization of Tall Cacti*, 13–15), and by R. Underhill (*The Autobiography of a Pápago Woman*, American Anthropological Association Memoir no. 46 [Washington, D.C., 1936], 10–11). For the Pima, the procedure is explained by Russell (*Pima Indians*, 71–72), and for the Maricopa, by L. Spier (*Yuman Tribes of the Gila River* [1933], 56–58).

7. Lumholtz (*New Trails in Mexico*, 120) observed the Papago at Santa Rosa mixing sahuaro syrup with one or two times its volume of water, while Castetter and Bell (*Aboriginal Utilization of Tall Cacti*, 22–23) mention for the same tribe that "it was mixed with four times the quantity of water, the ideal being a mild intoxicant which could be taken in quantity."

8. For the Papago, Lumholtz (*New Trails in Mexico*, 123) gives two days, the wine being ready on the third, while Castetter and Bell (*Aboriginal Utilization of Tall Cacti*, 23) cite seventy-two hours as the established fermenting time. Spier (*Yuman Tribes*, 57) gives two days for the Maricopa.

9. Hrdlička, *Physiological and Medical Observations*, 28.

10. Castetter and Bell, *Aboriginal Utilization of Tall Cacti*, 23.

11. Spier, *Yuman Tribes*, 57.

12. Castetter and Bell, *Aboriginal Utilization of Tall Cacti*, 23.

13. Standley (*Trees and Shrubs of Mexico*, 907) states: "The name 'pitahaya' (also written 'pitajaya' and 'pitaya') is generally employed in Mexico for fruits of cacti of the *Cereus* alliance. . . . The name of the State of . . . Sinaloa is said to be derived from two Indian words, 'sina,' *pitahaya*, and 'lobala,' round."

14. Oviedo, *Historia general*, vol. 3.

15. Castetter and Bell, *Aboriginal Utilization of Tall Cacti*, 28.

16. I. Pfefferkorn, *Beschreibung der Landschaft Sonora* (Cologne, 1794), 140.

17. Castetter and Bell, *Aboriginal Utilization of Tall Cacti*, 29, 30; [Nentvig], *Rudo ensayo*, 47.

18. Standley, *Trees and Shrubs*, 898–901.

19. According to N. L. Britton and G. N. Rose ("Cactaceae," *in* Standley, *Trees and Shrubs*, 865), a nopal is any member of the subgenus *Platyopuntia*.

20. At least half a dozen nopales with edible (and fermentable) tunas are indicated for Sonora and Sinaloa. Among the possibilities are *Opuntia gosseliniana*, *O. engelmannii*, *O. discata*, *O. chlorotica*, and *O. wilcoxii*, as described in Standley (*Trees and Shrubs*, 881–85), as well as *O. spraguei* and *O. rileyi*, as treated by H. Bravo, *Las Cactaceas de México* (Mexico, 1937), 176–78.

21. Pfefferkorn, *Beschreibung*, 137–38.

22. A. Hrdlička, "Notes on the Indians of Sonora, Mexico," *American Anthropologist*, n.s., 6 (1904): 73.

23. Hrdlička, *Physiological and Medical Observations*, 28.

24. [Nentvig], *Rudo ensayo*, 82.

25. Hrdlička, *Physiological and Medical Observations*, 28.

26. Memorias par la historia de Sinaloa, *Carta anua* (1593), p. 26.

27. [Nentvig], *Rudo ensayo*, 54, 82.

28. Ibid., 54.

29. Pfefferkorn, *Beschreibung*, 94, 140.

30. F. B. Kniffen, *Lower California Studies*. III: *The Primitive Cultural Landscape of the Colorado Delta*, University of California Publications in Geography 5, no. 2 (Berkeley, 1931), 53.

31. J. G. Bourke, "The Folk-Foods of the Rio Grande Valley and of Northern Mexico," *Journal of American Folklore* 8 (1895): 50.

32. Second anonymous [witness], *in* J. García Icazbalcéta, *Col. de doc. hist. de Méx.*, vol. 2, 303. It is impossible to tell from the account whether the mesquite drink was allowed to ferment or not, but A. Perez de Ribas (*Historia de los trivmphos de nvestra Santa Fe . . .* [Madrid, 1645]) specifically mentions a fermented mesquite beverage.

33. Perez de Ribas, *Historia*, vol. 2, 9.

CHAPTER 4

1. Academia de la Historia (Madrid), *Relación geográfica* for Chilchota, Michoacan, October 15, 1579, MS 12-18-3, no. 16, doc. 6, 22 ff. Photographic copy at the University of California; also *in* F. del Paso y Troncoso, *Papeles*, transcript copy in the Museo Nacional de México (part of unpublished tomo 8, vols. 1 and 2). Photographic copy at the University of California.

2. P. Beaumont, *Crónica de Michoacán* (eighteenth century), Publicaciones del Archivo General de la Nación, 3 vols. (Mexico City, 1932). Beaumont states (vol. 3, 462): "These

Indians [of Michoacán] made many alcoholic beverages by the fermentation of the grains of this plant [maize]. The various methods are recorded in the *Teatro Botánico* of Gaspar Balchino [*sic*]."

Beaumont's statement must be considered as undocumented, however, for Caspar Bauhin (*Teatri Botanici* [Basel, 1623], 25) makes only the vaguest of references to corn chicha as used in Peru, and has nothing to say about Michoacán. The earliest and most reliable account of Tarascan culture makes no mention of intoxicating beverages from maize, although wines from maguey, plums (*Spondias* sp.), and honey are listed (Col. doc. inéd. . . . España, "*Relación de las ceremonias y ritos, población y gobierno de los indios de la provincia de Mechoacan*," vol. 53, 69 [Madrid, 1842–1895]).

3. W. Jimenez Moreno, *Mapa lingüistico de Norte y Centro-América* (Mexico, 1936). The report of the *visita*, an apparently unknown document, was found and photographed by me in 1939. It is located in Guadalajara in the Archivo de Instrumentos Públicos de Jalisco, Ramo de Tierras y Aguas, libro 1, no. 3.

4. Neither Arias y Saavedra (*Informe* [1673], *in* A. Santoscoy, "*Nayarit*," *Colección de documentos inéditos, históricos y etnográficos* [Guadalajara, 1899]) nor Ortega (*Apostólicos afánes de la Compañia de Jesus* [Barcelona, 1754]) makes any mention of *tesgüino* among the Cora. The detailed reports from the Cora missions of 1777 (Biblioteca Nacional de México, *Relación geográfica* for the Cora mission, Jesús María y José, 1777, MS 15-3-76) are likewise silent on the subject, though other intoxicating drinks are mentioned. Herein we find a significant cultural difference between the Huichol and the Cora (see chapter 8).

5. Perez de Ribas, *Historia*, 574.

6. G. de Figueroa, *Puntos de anua de estos diez años que he asistido en este partido de San Pablo* (1662), *in* Documentos para la historia de Méjico, 4th series, vol. 3, 219.

7. K. T. Preuss, "*Der Ursprung der Religion und Kunst*," *Globus* 87 (1905): 418; Lumholtz, *Unknown Mexico*, vol. 1, 255.

8. Biblioteca Nacional de México, Letter of Estteuan Lorenzo to the viceroy, December 10, 1790, MS, legajo 93, no. 3, ff. 102–18 v.

9. Sauer, "Aboriginal Tribes and Languages," 55–56.

10. Lumholtz, *New Trails*, vol. 1, 255.

11. Memorias para la historia de Sinaloa, *Carta anua* (1593), p. 26.

12. J. F. Velasco, *Noticias estadísticas de Sonora* (Mexico, 1850), 74.

13. Siméon, *Dictionnaire* (Paris, 1885), 189, 412.

14. In the *relación geográfica* of Pópulo Gueguachic, Nueva Viscaya, dated December 4, 1777 (*in* Paso y Troncoso, *Papeles*, transcripts in Museo Nacional de México, legajo 4, no. 41), there is reference to "a corn drink that they call '*xuhuiqui*' and the *Mexicanos* '*texuino*.'" The author signs himself "Padre Mariano."

15. Bennett and Zingg, *Tarahumara*, 46, 149.

16. G. Mendoza, "*Sendechó*," *Boletín de la Sociedad Mexicana de Geografía y Estadística*, 2d epoca, 2 (1870): 25–28; Orozco y Berra, *Historia antigua*, vol. 1, 331.

17. J. Soustelle, *La famille Otomi-Pami du Mexique Central* (Paris, 1937), 512.

18. Juan de Velasco, *Historia del Reino de Quito* (1789) (Quito, 1844), vol. 1, 20.

19. Bennett and Zingg, *Tarahumara*, 46.

20. Further light on the use of this plant is shed by the *relación geográfica* of Pópulo Gueguachic (see note 14, above). The author writes that the grass is a native, uncultivated plant similar to oats and that the Tarahumar call it *basiahueque*. It is sometimes eaten for

food, dry and toasted, or is ground, mixed with water, and drunk as a gruel. There are two kinds: the one with white grains, called "*temivali*," and the other with red grains, called "*chullaca*." These seeds, he says, are added to the *xuhuiqui* (*tesgüino*) to make it stronger.

The precise function of the grass is difficult to discern, unless it improves the flavor. The idea that the grass would not ferment if cooked is probably superstition. Such a result would be expected only if the brome seeds were the only means whereby organisms responsible for the fermentation were introduced into the mixture. That, however, is not the case, as we are informed in the quotation from Bennett and Zingg that the Indians use the same fermenting vessel over and over without bothering to clean it (*Tarahumara*, 46). Most *tesgüino* brewers do not use brome grass.

Professor Joslyn (see chapter 1, note 1) believes that the grass may contain activators for the fermentation of maltose sugars present in the brew and that it may serve as a source of bios factors for the fermentation organisms.

21. According to Bennett and Zingg: "[T]hey often get drunk on cold nights, lose their blankets, and even fall asleep out on the trails in the bitter cold weather. Many catch pneumonia, which they attempt to guard against in typical primitive fashion by enlisting the aid of this harmless plant" (*Tarahumara*, 47).

22. How this procedure could produce "the effects of distillation" or in any way significantly increase the concentration of alcohol is hard to imagine.

23. Lumholtz, *Unknown Mexico*, vol. 2, 186–87.

24. Mendoza, "*Sendechó*," 25.

25. I was unable to ascertain this point, since the use of these leaves is no longer considered a necessary step in making *sendechó*.

26. Mendoza states ("*Sendechó*," 25): "Once dried, they reduce it to a thick powder in a mill together with the corn, or then add an amount of red chilies, without observing the exact measurement; but that can be figured six or eight portions for a third of the corn."

27. Ibid.

28. The analysis of a similar product gave 0.7 to 0.9 percent alcohol and 1.4 to 1.9 percent unfermented sugar (E. Gonzalez, *Análisis del Tejuino*, MS in the Escuela de Farmacía, Universidad de Guadalajara, Mexico).

29. Lumholtz, *Unknown Mexico*, vol. 2, 186. In English the name of the fruit has been corrupted into "guava."

30. Juan Navarro's report of 1784, *in* M. Orozco y Berra, *Apéndice al diccionario universal de historia y de geografía*, tomo 1 (8 of the work), Mexico, 1855

31. I. Dávila Garibi, *Breves apuntes acerca de los Chimalhuacanos* (Guadalajara, 1927), 187. The place is recorded on most maps as Tepechitlán and is located just south of Tlaltenango, Zacatecas.

CHAPTER 5

1. Mota y Escobar records that those members of the tribe of "*Mexues y Ocolas*" who lived along the Rio de la Nazas planted maize along its seasonally flooded banks (A. de la Mota y Escobar, *Descripción Geográfica de los Reynos de Galicia, Vizcaya, y Leon* [1602–1605 ?; Mexico, 1930], 155).

2. For the region around Cerralvo in Nuevo Leon, Alonso de León makes the comment that the best of the tunas found there are not as good as the worst of Nueva España (*in* G. García and C. Pereyra, *Doc. inéd. ó muy raros hist. Méj.*, vol. 25, 37–38).

3. *In* F. Orozco y Jiménez, *Col. doc. hist. inéd.* . . . *Arzobispo, Guadalajara*, vol. 5, no. 1 (Guadalupe, January 1, 1926), 102–16. The name is here spelled Ahumada.

4. *In* H. Trimborn, *Quellen zur Kulturgeschichte des präkolumbischen Amerika* (Stuttgart, 1936), 162.

5. Gonzales de la Casas is probably guilty of an inaccuracy here. These nomads almost certainly did not make pulque, but fermented a drink out of baked mescal. Only strictly sedentary groups can ordinarily make pulque, for its preparation entails two or three times a day tapping the same plant, which then quickly decays. Furthermore, Trimborn (ibid., 161) stated previously that "they eat the leaves and the root baked in an oven. [This food] is here called "*mixcali*," and it is good, and of it they make wine which they drink."

6. For example, A. Maurizio declares: "Without jars . . . fermented drinks are not represented" (*Geschichte der gegorenen Getränke* [Berlin, 1933], 1).

7. J. Arlegui, *Chronica de la Provincia de N.S.P.S., Francisco de Zacatecas* (Mexico, 1737), 160.

8. Juan de Cardenas, *Problemas y secretos maravillosos de las Indias* (1st ed., Mexico, 1591; 2d ed., Mexico, 1913), 182–83.

9. The information is based partially on fieldwork in San Luis Potosí and Aguascalientes in December 1938 and partially on the following authorities: (1) D. Griffiths and R. F. Hare, *Prickly Pear and Other Cacti as Food for Stock*, New Mexico Agricultural Experiment Station Bulletin no. 60 (Albuquerque, November 1906); (2) R. F. Hare and D. Griffiths, *The Tunas as a Food for Man*, New Mexico Agricultural Experiment Station Bulletin no. 64 (Albuquerque, April 1907); (3) N. L. Britton and G. N. Rose, "Cactaceae," in Standley, *Trees and Shrubs of Mexico*, Contributions from the U.S. National Herbarium no. 23 (Washington, D.C., 1924), 855–1012; (4) N. L. Britton and G. N. Rose, *The Cactaceae*, 4 vols. (Washington, D.C., 1919–1923); (5) L. Diguet, *Les Cactacées Utiles du Mexique* (Paris, 1928); (6) H. Bravo, *Las cactaceas de Mexico* (Mexico, 1937).

10. It extends from Texas to Oaxaca, and is especially plentiful from Durango to Querétaro (L. Diguet, *Les Cactacées utiles du Mexique* [Paris, 1928], 112).

11. F. X. Alegre, *Historia de la Compañia de Jesús en Nueva España*, Bustamente edition, 3 vols. (Mexico, 1841), vol. 1, 281.

12. Coxcatlán lies near Tehuacán, Puebla, and does not belong in the tuna and mesquite region because the common drink in the neighborhood is pulque. But since the *relación* gives some additional information about tuna wine, it was thought best to include the quotation here. The document seen was a manuscript copy made by Paso y Troncoso (*Papales*, transcript in Museo Nacional de México, part of unpublished tomo 8, vols. 1 and 2, photographic copy at the University of California, Berkeley).

13. *In* M. Orozco y Berra, *Apéndice al Diccionario Universal de Historia y de Geografía*, tomo 1, vol. 8 of the work (Mexico, 1855), 354–62.

14. Hare, Mitchell, and Bjerregaard, *Denatured Alcohol*.

15. The *colonche* made nowadays around San Luis Potosí is usually stronger than this because the cactus juice is boiled for two or three hours before fermentation and thus concentrated into a stronger must. The mixture is usually either seeded with some old *colonche* or has some of the fruit rinds thrown in, which seem to harbor the fermenting organisms.

16. Formerly known as *P. juliflora*. Cf. Standley, *Trees and Shrubs*, 1567.

17. Ibid., 352.

18. Wooden mortars were often used in other regions for pounding the fibrous mesquite pods, as they were found by experience to work better than stone mortars. Precise data regarding mortars in this area have not been found.

19. *Mizquitamalli* was prepared by the Chichimeca for use during the season of scarcity ("Certain breads that they stored for the course of a year") according to Aumada. *In* Orosco y Jeménez, *Col. doc. hist. inéd. . . . Arzobispo*, vol. 5, no. 1, 102–16.

20. Mota y Escobar, *Descripción geográfica*.

21. B. de Sahagún, *Historia general de las cosas de Nueva España* (Mexico, 1938), vol. 3, 226.

22. Hrdlička, *Notes*.

23. The name "peyote" (Nahuatl *peyotl*) refers specifically to *Lophophora williamsii*, a small, spineless, turniplike cactus, of which only the roundish, ribbed, tufted top appears above ground. The top alone is edible, either fresh or dried or ground with water, and contains a number of alkaloids of varying physiological effects. The main result of peyote consumption appears to be visual hallucinations, accompanied by nausea and various other physical and psychological derangements. For details and bibliography, see W. La Barre, *The Peyote Cult*, Yale University Publications in Anthropology no. 19 (New Haven, Connecticut, 1938).

24. Sahagún, *Historia general*, vol. 3, 118.

25. In certain areas peyote and alcoholic drinks were taken together, at times actually mixed in the same concoction. The consumption of both peyote and *tesgüino* is a ritualistic necessity at certain Huichol and Tarahumar festivals. According to Cenobio Crux (personal communication), ex-gobernador of the Tuxpan (Jalisco) Huichol, whom I visited in December 1938, peyote is never actually mixed in the *tesgüino*, though R. M. Zingg (*The Huichols: Primitive Artists*, Contributions to Ethnography no. 1 [New York, 1938], 195) records a tradition to this effect.

The *relación geográfica* for San Miguel el Grande, Obispado de Michoacán, of August 30, 1777 (Biblioteca Nacional de México, MS 15-3-76) contains the following:

> Pellote. Species of biznaga, downy and woolly, which the Indians use a great deal in pulque, to which it gives a strong flavor, with which they easily intoxicate themselves. They say that their fantasy is affected, so that they see many visions.

(San Miguel el Grande is located in the state of Guanajuato. The Indians are Otomí.)

Hartwich (*Menschlichen Genussmittel*, 249) mentions an alleged drink of the Tarahumar, as recorded in the eighteenth century, in which ground peyote is fermented(!). To the resulting liquor are added tobacco leaves. The recipe sounds very potent, but it is doubtful if real fermentation is involved, since the peyote cactus contains very little directly fermentable material.

26. Cf. map in G. Wagner, "Entwicklung und Verbreitung des Peyote-Kultes," *Baessler Archiv* 15 (1932):59–141.

27. Santa Maria, *Relación histórica*, 399, 406–7.

28. A. de León, *in* García and Pereyra, *Doc. inéd.*, 42–45.

29. That peyote was introduced into the *tesgüino* region from the east is at once evident: *Lophophora* does not grow wild in the Sierra Madre Occidental and the peyote-using tribes go to great pains to get it. The Tarahumara generally obtain it from the neighborhood of the Conchos–Rio Grande confluence (Bennett and Zingg, *Tarahumara*, 136), whereas the Huichol make an even longer pilgrimage to the hills around Catorce, San Luis Potosí, into the heart of the land of their relatives (ancestors?), the Guachichil. The Cora occasionally plant peyote, as C. Lumholtz observed (*Unknown Mexico*, vol. 1, 509).

30. Sahagún, *Historia general*; F. Hernandez, *Nova plantarvm, animalivm et mineralivm Mexicanorvm* (Rome ed., 1651; Madrid ed., 1790), F. Ximénez, trans., 2d ed. (Morelia, Mexico, 1838).

CHAPTER 6

1. Hernán Cortés, "Second Letter to Charles V, October 30, 1520," *Cartas de relación de la conquista de Méjico*, Calpé ed. (Madrid, 1922), vol. 1, 99.

They sell honey and wax from bees and syrup from cornstalks, which is as pleasing and sweet as that from sugar, and syrup from plants that these people and others call "*maguey*," that is much better when boiled down. And they make sweetenings and wine from these plants, that are themselves sold.

2. *Relación de las ceremonias*, in Col. doc. inéd. . . . hist. de España, vol. 53, 16: "There are . . . important stewards for receiving and guarding all of the syrup from cornstalks and bees that is turned into sugar."

3. Garcilaso de la Vega, *Primera parte de los comentarios reales* (Lisbon, 1609; Madrid, 1723), 277.

4. Waugh, *Iroquois Foods*, 101, 146.

5. Bennett and Zingg, *Tarahumara*, 47.

6. Lumholtz, *Unknown Mexico*, vol. 1, 257.

7. Navarro was Director General de Alcabalas y Pulques in the administration of Gálvez. The report is dated February 29, 1784, and is a comprehensive survey of types of alcoholic beverages used in towns where tax offices were located. *In* Orozco y Berra, *Apéndice*, tomo 1, 354–62.

8. Archivo General de la Nación, México, *Ramo de Ordenanzas*, vol. 2, 207v–8. Mexico City.

9. *In* Orozco y Berra, *Apéndice*, tomo 1, 454–62.

10. F. del Paso y Troncoso, *Papeles*, 2d series, vol. 5, 101.

11. Used in the sense of non-Aztec, but Nahua-speaking.

12. This material, known in Totonaco as "*limacatlín*," is the root or bark of a shrub or small tree with a white flower, whose Totonac name is "*tzutzún*." A similar red-flowered plant is not used. From a sample of leaves, flowers, and pods I brought back, the plant has been tentatively identified by Professor H. L. Mason of the Department of Botany of the University of California as *Calliandra laxa*. The product is closely related to a number of herbs used in making pulque in Oaxaca, where the names "*timbre*," "*timbe*," and "*timbrillo*" are also applied. For a further discussion of *timbre*, see Appendix B.

13. A *manojo* in this case is a small bundle of the root or bark of *limacatlín* weighing about an ounce. In Zapotitlán only the root is used, whereas in Zongozotla, two miles away, the bark is favored. This differentiation may not be significant.

14. C. Patiño, *Vocabulario Totonaco* (Xalapa, 1907), 16.

15. The Navarro document does not mention which group uses the beverage (*in* Orozco y Berra, *Apéndice*, tomo 1, 354–62). It may quite possibly be Tepehua.

CHAPTER 7

1. F. López de Gómara, *Historia de México*, 2d ed. (Anvers, 1554), 344v.

2. J. C. Segura (*El maguey*, 4th ed. [Mexico, 1901], 18–19) presents an alternative explanation. He recalls that a certain rodent called "*metoro*" is very common in maguey plantings and that it habitually punctures the hearts of the ripe magueys in order to drink the juice. Perhaps, he conjectures, somebody may have observed the animal on some occasion in

the dim past and have tasted the juice flowing from the puncture and found it good, especially if it had already fermented a little. The pulque process is then supposed to have been learned through conscious imitation and gradual improvement of techniques. The argument has the weakness of assuming that man did not utilize the magueys for food before he discovered how to make pulque—a most unlikely assumption.

3. This part of the procedure would account for the sparse record concerning the utilization of the pulque maguey shoots for food. In addition to the Gómara account, I know of only one other explicit statement regarding the simultaneous use of the shoot and the sap, namely that of the *relación* of Chiconauhtla of January 4, 1580 (Paso y Troncoso, *Papeles*, 2d series, vol. 6, 172: "There are a great many trees that they call '*maguey*,' from which wine and vinegar are produced and jam is made from the heart." Chiconauhtla is located in the Valley of Mexico just north of Lake Texcoco. The *relación* of Tepeaca (*in* Paso y Troncoso, *Papeles*, 2d series, vol. 5, 36) mentions that the flower shoot is cut, but says nothing about baking it for food. A great many of the *relaciones* record the baking of the thick leaf bases, a process that did not significantly diminish the total quantity of aguamiel available.

4. This number is not to be taken literally. It seems to mean an indefinite large number in Nahua symbolism. Sahagún explains that there was supposed to be a different god for all the various effects the intoxication produced in different individuals (*Historia general* [Mexico, 1938], vol. 1, 313–15; vol. 2, 236).

5. E. G. Seler, *Gesammelte Abhandlungen zur Amerikanischen Sprach und Alterumskunde*, vol. 2, 92: "*Das Pulquegefäss der Bilimek'schen Sammlung.*"

6. C. de Tapia Zenteno, *Noticia de la lengua Huasteca* (Mexico, 1767).

7. E. Mendieta Huerta, "*La economía de los pueblos indígenas huastecos de San Luis Potosí,*" *Revista Mexicana de Sociología* 2 (1939): 59.

8. Listed in the 1784 Navarro report for Tampico (*in* Orozco y Berra, *Apéndice*, tomo 1). The beverage does not seem to be recorded earlier for the Huaxtec region, but the Pánuco *relación* of 1609 (*in* Col. doc. inéd . . . ultramar, vol. 9, 141) mentions that palm cabbage is used for food. That being the case, the aboriginal manufacture of palm wine is very probable.

9. Sahagún, *Historia general*, vol. 3, 139.

10. Seler, *Gesammelte Abhandlungen*, especially vol. 2, 169: "*Die alten Ansiedlungen im Gebiete der Huaxteca*"; vol. 2, 923–24: "*Das Pulquefäss der Bilimek'schen Sammlung*"; and vol. 3, 249: "*Die Pauke von Malinalco und das Zeichen Atl-tlachinolli.*" See also his article, "*Die Wandskulpturen im Tempel des Pulquegottes von Tepoztlan.*" Congrès International des Américanistes, 1906, vol. 2 (Québec, 1907), 351–79.

11. This *relación* has not been published and I have not seen it. The copy that formerly belonged to García Icazbalceta is now presumably in the collection of the University of Texas. The legend was commented on by Seler (*Wandskulpturen*, vol. 2, 351–79) and by F. Plancarte y Navarrete (*Prehistoria de México* [Tlalpam, D.F., 1923], 651).

A curious statement in the "First anonymous [witness]" (*in* J. García Icazbalceta, *Col. doc. hist. de Méx.*, vol. 2 [Mexico, 1858–1866], 295) referring to the Nahua population not far north of Metztitlán substantiates our views regarding the ritualistic importance of pulque in this area:

> The village that is found in the valleys of the Huasteca is San Luis . . . twenty leagues from the city of Pánuco. . . . The Indians make a very large amount of pulque from their magueys, which is the wine that they drink. When they are intoxicated and at festivals, they no longer can drink with their mouths, so they lie down with a sucking tube.

12. *Relaciones geográficas* of 1609 *in* Col. de doc. inéd . . . ultramar, vol. 9, 133–66. For Pánuco, p. 141: "pulque, wine, and drink that they make from maguey sap"; for Tanteyuc (Tantoyuca), p. 147: "drinks they call 'pulque' that they make from the sap of a tree they call 'maguey'." Somewhere in the Pánuco lowlands, Cortés found certain stores of wine which may have been pulque (recorded in his fourth letter of October 15, 1524 (*Cartas*, vol. 2, 81).

13. This point was mentioned in chapter 2. It is a given that a maguey from which sap is being collected must be tapped two or three times a day for from two to six months; if the tapping is not carried out consistently and the central cavity not scraped clean each time, the plant rots. Not only does the sedentariness of the pulque producers imply agriculture for food supply but also the utilization of the maguey for pulque practically imposes the necessity of maguey planting, since natural stands are almost invariably sparse or, alternatively, are in rocky country of such high relief that settlements are unlikely.

14. There is reason to believe that this may have been precisely what happened to differentiate the economy of the Mazahua and Otomí from that of the Pame, their linguistic relatives. The former were contiguous to the Nahua groups (Toltec; "Chichimec"—in the historical sense of the Mesa Central; Aztec) and were at various times under partial or complete Nahua domination. The Pame never had the advantage of close contact with the higher southern culture. They did, however, adopt the use of those alcoholic stimulants that would still leave them their mobility.

Payne (*History*, 405) is probably right in seeing the presence of the pulque maguey on the plain of Anáhuac as providing much of the attractive force that resulted in the repeated influx of barbarous tribes from outside, of which the Aztec intrusion was merely the most recent and best remembered.

15. The Jiménez Moreno linguistic map (*Mapa lingüistico*) shows the Pame language for all of the present state of Querétaro except for the extreme southern tip. On that basis, the area would fall into the tuna and mesquite region. However, the 1582 *relación* for Querétaro (*in* G. Velázques, *Colección . . . San Luis Potosí*, vol. 1, 1–48) is explicit in making the site of the settlement aboriginally Otomí, and describes a complete pulque complex, including the use of "pulque roots."

16. *Relación* for Nuchistlan and Suchipila *in* Paso y Troncoso, *Papales* (transcript in the Museo Nacional, Mexico, part of unpublished tomo 8), vol. 1; *Relación* for Taltenango, ibid.

17. Mota y Escobar, *Descripción geográfica*, 121–22.

18. As indicated in chapter 4, note 3, I found and photographed this apparently unknown document in 1939. It is a report of the *visita* to Nueva Galicia of the *oidor* Daualos y Toledo in 1616, and is located in Guadalajara in the Archivo de Instrumentos Públicos de Jalisco, Ramo de Tierras y Aguas, libro 1, no. 3.

19. Mota y Escobar refers to "heathen Chichimecas" (Zapotec?) in connection with Colotlan, making it appear as though only they were involved (*Descripción geográfica*, 125.) This is not the case, however, as Daualos y Toledo mentions for Colotlan a "barrio of Chichimecas," a "barrio of Tlaxcaltecas," and a "barrio of Tochos" (Cazcan) (see note 18, above).

20. In Santoscoy, "*Nayarit*," 25. For example, the *relación* for Citlaltomagua (Guerrero) of 1580 (*in* Paso y Troncoso, *Papeles*, 2d series, vol. 6, 163) uses the word "pulque" with reference to wines from canes (sugar? maize?), pineapples, bananas, and plums. A similar case even more to the point is the report in the "Third anonymous [witness]" published by García Icazbalceta (*Col. doc. hist. de Méx.*, vol. 2, 451). For the town of Pochotla, Province of Piastla (southern Sinaloa) the author states: "They make much pulque from mescal and plums." The locality

referred to is near the seacoast, and the author complains of the great heat. This climate is obviously not the kind where pulque magueys would thrive, and the term "pulque from mescal" must be equated with mescal wine. Some confusion has arisen in the literature from this loose terminology. See C. Sauer and D. Brand, "Aztatlán," *Ibero-Americana* 1 (1932): 53.

21. Ortega, *Apostólicos afanes*, 21; J. de Ortega, *Vocabulario en lengua castellana y cora* (1732): "*Maguei. Yuchit*"; "*Vino mixcal. Nahuáti.*"

22. Biblioteca Nacional de México, *Relación geográfica* for the Cora Missions, 1777.

23. L. Diguet, "*La Sierra du Nayarit et ses indigènes,*" *Nouvelles archives des missions scientifiques* 9 (1899): 571–630. The beverage obtained is of the inferior *tlachique* variety (p. 585).

24. *Relación geográfica* for Autlán *in* Paso y Troncoso, *Papales* (transcript in the Museo Nacional de México, part of unpublished tomo 8).

25. The *relación* of 1580 for "Quacoman" mentions syrup and wine from magueyes (*in* ibid., tomo 8, vol. 2).

26. The neighborhood of Ichcateopan appears to represent the only aboriginal extension of pulque into the confines of the present state of Guerrero. The people of the region spoke Chontal, but were vassals to the Aztecs, who had built their biggest frontier fort against the Tarascans at the settlement of Oztuma, six leagues east of Ichcateopan (*Relación geográfica* for Ichcateopan, 1580, *in* Paso y Troncoso, *Papeles*, 2d series, vol. 6, 110).

27. Tepoztlán was the sacred place of Tepoztecatl, one of the most important regional pulque divinities in Nahua mythology. The impressive ruins of the subpyramidal temple still stand on a steep hill overlooking the town. The site was intensively studied by Seler (*Wandskulpturen*, vol. 2, 351–79). It seems curious that the temple of this very important incarnation of Ometuchtli should be located in a place that is distinctly marginal to the pulque area. The *relación* of 1580 does mention the manufacture of pulque and maguey syrup (*in* Paso y Troncoso, *Papeles*, 2d series, vol. 6, 247), but it no longer is. Redfield states that the "maguey does not flourish at this low altitude; therefore *pulque* . . . must be imported, and its use is confined largely to festal occasions" (R. Redfield, *Tepoztlan, A Mexican Village* [Chicago, 1930], 42).

It would seem that the pre-Columbian pulque region had advanced beyond its natural limits in a number of places. The case of Pánuco has already been discussed. A similar state of affairs held true at Jalapa, Veracruz, where pulque was manufactured in pre-Conquest times and was still recorded in the 1580 *relación* (*in* Paso y Troncoso, *Papeles*, 2d series, vol. 5, 101) and in the Navarro report of 1784 (*in* Orozco y Berra, *Apéndice*, tomo 1), but where it has now disappeared. The coming of the railroad made it possible to bring in much better pulque from the neighborhood of Perote, 4,000 feet higher, on the edge of the plateau.

28. This statement is confirmed in M. Martínez Gracida, *Historia antigua de la Chontalpa Oaxaqueña*, Sociedad Científica "Antonio Alzate" Memoria no. 30, 83 (Mexico City, 1910). Farther to the east and south, in Chiapas and Guatemala, the pulque complex was introduced in the early colonial period through the resettling of Indians from the Mexican plateau. The "spot settling" of nuclei of trusted Indians into remote regions was an important part of early Spanish colonial policy, and we have already encountered it in the case of the Tlaxcalan garrison at Colotlan. Alonso Ponce visited Guatemala in the late 1580s and observed that there were Mexican magueys in the vicinity of Almolonga that had been planted by the newcomers (*Viaje a Nueva España*, vol. 1 [Mexico, 1947], 241).

> There were some magueys . . . planted by Mexicans who came with the Spaniards after the Conquest, one group was from Tlatilolco, others from Xuchimilco, or from

Tepeaco . . . and there were also others who were Tlascaltecan, but all of them there were called "Mexicans."

A century later, Fuentes y Guzmán informs us that of the twenty-eight towns in the neighborhood of Guatemala City, Almolonga and San Gaspar were most famous for their production of pulque (*Recordación florida: Discurso historial* . . . , Biblioteca "Goathemala" de la Sociedad de Geográfica e Historia, vol. 6 in 3 vols. [Guatemala, 1932–1933], vol. 2, 214). A similar introduction took place into Chiapas where the Tzotzil (Chamula) Indians of the highlands still make pulque today, though their process shows certain modifications. For example, instead of drawing out the aguamiel with a gourd pipette, they use bowls to dip it out.

29. The large size of these plants is apparently not the result of crossbreeding, since the process of aguamiel extraction literally nips in the bud the sexually reproductive parts of the plant. Reproduction results from the budding of suckers from the root stock. Hence, crossbreeding is out of the question, and the plant cannot be considered as domesticated in a biological sense.

30. *Memoria instructiva sobre el maguey o Agave mexicano* (Mexico, 1837). The author of this work writes under the egalitarian pseudonym of "El Ciudadano José Ramo Zeschan Noamira"; his actual name is José Mariano Sánchez y Mora, Conde del Peñasco. The listing of these varieties and illustrations of their leaf profiles are reprinted in the more easily accessible work of Segura (*Maguey*, 36–41, plates 1–6).

31. A. Ramírez Laguna, *Distribución de los agaves de México*, Anales del Instituto de Biología (de la Universidad Nacional Autónoma) (Mexico, 1936), vol. 7, 17–45.

32. *In* Standley, *Trees and Shrubs*.

33. Berger, *Agaven*, 17.

34. Summarized from Sánchez y Mora (*in* Standley, *Trees and Shrubs*).

35. H. Ruiz de Alarcon, *Tratado de las idolatrías, supersticiones, dioses, ritos, hechicerías y otras costumbres gentílicas* . . . (1629), *Anales del Museo Nacional Mexico*, 1st época, vol. 6, 127–223 (Mexico City, 1892, 1900).

36. Sahagún (*Historia general*, vol. 1, 113, 126) mentions that pulque was drunk through hollow canes and that canes were similarly used by priests to draw blood from the bleeding gashes in the chests of sacrificial victims after their hearts had been cut out. These canes were called "*acocotli*" and were probably the hollowed-out stems of *Arracacia atropurpurea* (W. Gates, *The De la Cruz-Vadiano Aztec Herbal of 1552*, The Maya Society Publication no. 23 [Baltimore, 1939], 121; Robelo, *Diccionario* [Cuernavaca, 1904], 1; Martínez, *Catálogo* [Mexico, 1937], 12). (See text for use of gourd pipettes, called "*ococote*," made from *Lagenaria vulgaris*; also note 38, below.)

37. Segura, *Maguey*.

38. *Lagenaria vulgaris*, unquestionably native to the Old World, naturalized itself in the American tropics at some remote prehistoric period. The woody, buoyant fruit was well suited to transportation by water and was apparently transported, like the coconut, through the agency of ocean currents. Unlike the coconut, however, it had by the time of the Conquest achieved a wide distribution in the New World and had entered significantly into the ecology of many American tribes, partially a reflection, no doubt, of its earlier arrival. The gourds used for extracting aguamiel were imported into the pulque region from the lowlands.

39. E. Palacios, *El alcoholismo en el problema indígena de México*, Boletín de la Sociedad Mutualista Médico-Farmaceutica de Guadalajara 9 (1937): 261–80.

40. The steps taken to ferment aguamiel are explained in detail by Segura (*Maguey*) and others. Basic work on the microbiology of the fermentation process was done by Paul Lindner. See his *Mikroskopische und biologische Betriebskontrolle in dem Gärungsgewerbe, sechste neubearbeitete Auflage* (Berlin, 1930), especially 581–93 on *Agavengärungen*. The most intensive researches have been carried on in the last five years by the staff of the Instituto de Biología, Universidad Nacional de México, and are being published in the Anales del Instituto de Biología.

41. These figures are given by F. Bulnes (*El pulque e studio científico* [Mexico, 1909], 3–4). There is a reason to believe that his acid value is too low. I have not been able to locate reliable recent analyses of pulque. Palacios (*Alcoholismo*, 275) cites a recent determination of 4.47 parts per thousand, of which 3.12 is fixed acid (expressed as lactic acid). It is of course true that acidity increases sharply with age, but the fermentation of pulque is by no means a simple yeast fermentation, and the acidity values should be fairly high all along. Lobato (*Estudio quimico-industrial de los varios productos del maguey mexicana* [Mexico, 1884], 98–124) gives total acidities of 0.3 or 0.4 percent. But his analyses are not reliable, as he invariably finds the alcohol content of his samples to be around 8 percent, a preposterous result even when 100 percent conversion of sugar is assumed, as Bulnes (*Pulque*, 63) was one of the first to point out.

42. A. J. Carbajal, *La fermentación racional del pulque*, Memorias de la Sociedad Científica "Antonio Alzate" Memoria no. 32, 224 (Mexico City, 1912).

43. López de Gómara, *Historia de México*, 319v.

44. Bulnes, *Pulque*, 26–28.

45. G. Fernandez Tagle, *Estudio de las vitaminas y de la fermentación viscosa en el pulque*, Universidad de México (1931); J. Roca and R. Llamas, "*Las vitaminas del pulque*," *Anales del Instituto de Biología* 9 (1938): 81–84.

Roca and Llamas found also, by means of chemical indicators, considerable quantities of vitamin C, although nutritional tests on guinea pigs as reported by Fernandez Tagle were negative.

46. P. Lindner, "*Das Geheimnis um Soma . . .*," *Forschungen und Fortschritte* 9 (1933): 65–66.

47. Sahagún, *Historia general*, vol. 3, 139.

48. T. Motolinía (*Memoriales* [Mexico, 1903], 313–14) is most emphatic that this is the true explanation of the great amount of drunkenness among the Indians.

49. As published in Vasco de Puga, *Provisiones, cédulas, instrucciones para el gobierno de la Nueva España* (Mexico, 1563; Madrid, 1945), f. 70:

> I [the Queen] am informed that the native Indians of New Spain have a certain wine they call "pulque." It is said, when they have their fiestas and at all other times of the year, they put a root . . . in the pulque to affect the processing of the wine and to fortify it and add more zest to it. . . . They become intoxicated . . . and as they become violent, they fight each other and some die. And afterward, the drunken words are very vicious and lustful. . . . And in order to remedy and change this, they should not gather such a root, but should gather some other thing that would not change the wine, and I would request it and also dispatch a order. Therefore, I order and commission you immediately to see to the aforesaid.

50. *Relación de Texcoco*, 1582, *in* J. García Icazbalceta, ed., *Nueva collección de documentos para la historia de México*, vol. 3, 65 (Mexico, 1886–1892).

51. A. L. Aguilar, "*El cuapatli ó madera del pulque*," *El Mexico antiguo* 2 (1924): 14, 18.

It should be pointed out that a town with the name of Zimapan is located not far from Metztitlán and is the probable site of the earliest use of pulque. "Zimapan" can be translated as "moist place where roots grow." Unfortunately, however, we can draw no inference from the location of this place-name. Zimapan is in too cold a location for the growth of pulque roots, and the 1579 *relación* for Zimapan (*in* Paso y Troncoso, *Papeles*, 2d series, vol. 6, 2) explains that the place was named after certain fleshy roots that grew in the hills and were used by the natives for food.

52. *Relación geográfica* for Atlatlauca y Malinaltepec, 1580 (*in* Paso y Troncoso, *Papeles*, 2d series, vol. 5, 171).

53. It seems odd that the Spanish word for cinnamon should have been applied to pulque root since there is very little resemblance. True *canela* (cinnamon) was occasionally added to pulque during the colonial period, and it may be that the word had its meaning gradually extended in vulgar usage to include any bark put into pulque. The addition to pulque of "something fragrant like cinnamon" is mentioned in a quaint manuscript of 1748 by C. F. de Torres (*Virtudes maravillosas de pulque, medicamento vniversal, ô polychresto*, MS 14-8-26, Biblioteca Nacional de México, Mexico City).

54. Aguilar, "*Cuapatli ó madera.*"

55. Standley, *Trees and Shrubs*, 381, 385.

56. Aguilar, "*Cuapatli ó madera*," 18–19.

57. One writer has actually claimed that *ocpatli* was nothing more than peyote, which is quite out of the question (H. B. Alexander, *Latin American Mythology* [Boston, 1920], 77).

58. A. Núñez de Haro y Peralta, "*Carta al juez de bebidas prohibidas*," July 3, 1777, MS 318, Biblioteca Nacional de México, Mexico City.

59. J. de la Barrera, [Report on prohibition, 1692], Museo Nacional de México, E.B.T. 2.336, ffl 48–53v.

60. The Nahuatl dialects did not use the 'r' sound. According to Gates (*Aztec Herbal*, xvi), a similar name, "*pelon camotli*," was given to *Solanum tuberosum*.

61. Hernández, *Nova plantarvm* (Rome, 1651), 54; (Madrid, 1790), vol. 1, 188; (2d ed., F. Ximénez, trans.), 23.

62. P. de Cieza de León, *Crónica del Peru* (Madrid, ca. 1922), 450.

63. Garcilaso de la Vega, *Primera parte de los commentarios*, 280.

64. See Paso y Troncoso, *Papeles*, transcript in the Museo Nacional de México, part of unpublished tomo 8.

65. *In* Orozco y Berra, *Apéndice*, tomo 1.

66. Ibid.

67. Ibid.

68. Cortés, "Second letter to Charles V, October 30, 1520," *Cartas*, vol. 1; *Codex Mendoza, Codice Mendocino*, "Mexico," phototypic ed. (1925), 27, 29.

69. Sahagún, *Historia general*, vol.3, 100.

70. *In* Paso y Troncoso, *Papeles*, 2d series, vol. 5, 186 (Cuicatlán, 1580), vol. 4 (Tepoztlán, Xalapa, Pánuco, 1579).

71. Sahagún (*Historia general*, vol. 1, 357) speaks of a city's baptismal rites at which both ordinary white pulque, *iztacoctli* (*iztac*, "white"), and *ayoctli* (evidently a variant of *aoctli*) were consumed.

72. *In* Paso y Troncoso, *Papeles*, 2d series, vol. 6, 310.

73. F. J. Clavigero, *Historia antigua de México y de su conquista* (Mexico, 1844).

74. Ibid.

75. R. E. Latcham, *La agricultura precolombiana en Chile . . .* (Santiago, 1936), 142–43.

76. Cortés uses the word "pulque" in a letter to the king, dated October 15, 1524. This is not the well-known "fourth letter" of the same date, but another, which García Icazbalceta terms "*carta inédita*" (in *Col. doc. hist. de Méx.*, vol. 1, 475). Rodrigo de Albornoz also uses the word in a letter to the Crown dated December 15, 1525 (ibid., vol. 1, 488). The first legal recognition of the word seems to come in the royal *cédula* of August 24, 1529 (Vasco de Puga, *Provisiones*).

77. L. Wiener, *Africa and the Discovery of America* (Philadelphia, 1920–1922), vol. 2, 114; A. Costa Alvarez, *El ultimo diccionario de la academia* (La Plata, 1925).

78. J. García Icazbalceta, *Obras* . . . (Mexico City, 1896–1899), vol. 6, 272.

79. *In* Segura, *Maguey*, 20–21; see also C. A. Robelo's excellent article on pulque (*Diccionario de Aztequismos* [Nueva Edición, 1912], 637–42).

80. Robelo, *Diccionario* (Nueva Edición, 1912).

81. Plancarte y Navarrete, *Prehistoria*, 666.

82. Robelo, *Diccionario* (Nueva Edición, 1912), 345.

83. This derivation, at least, is the opinion of Peñafiel, as cited in A. Genin, *La cerveza entre los antiguos mexicanos y en la actualidad* (Mexico, 1924), especially p. 10.

84. A. de Molina, *Vocabulario en lengua mexicana y castellana* . . . (Mexico, 1571).

85. Siméon, *Dictionnaire*, 486.

86. They were of course not plums at all, but members of the cashew family (Anacardiaceae), whereas true plums, genus *Prunus*, belong to the almond family (Amygdalaceae).

87. The taxonomic names given on pp. 656–57 of Standley (*Trees and Shrubs)* are amended on p. 1671.

88. For a good introduction to the subject of Nahua plant nomenclature, see the introduction to Gates (*Aztec Herbal*, especially v–xxv).

89. Sahagún, *Historia General*, vol. 3, 225–26.

90. Hernández, *Nova plantarvm*; F. Ximénez, *Quatro libros de la náturaleza* . . . (Mexico, 1888), 53 (*copalxocotl*), 175 (*guauhxocotl*, not recorded in modern botanical literature, may have been local usage around Cholula), 218 (*mexocotl*).

91. *Spondias purpurea* is less sensitive to cold than *S. mombin*, which has a more southerly distribution, especially along the Pacific Coast, and hence is not included in the present discussion of plants utilized for wine in the pulque area.

92. *In* Paso y Troncoso, *Papeles*, 2d series, vol. 6, 91 (Papaloticpac), vol. 6, 171 (Atlatlauaca y Malinaltepec), vol. 4, 186 (Cuicatlán).

93. Sahagún, *Historia general*, vol. 3, 226. It is of interest to note that one of the words for drunkenness in Nahuatl, a language singularly articulate on the general subject of intoxication, is derived from *xocotl*. The word is *xocomictia*, "to get or make drunk," derived from *xocotl*, "acidulous fruit," and *mictia*, "to kill" (cf. Mictlan, "Place of the dead"). There were three main linguistic roots for drunkenness, each of which could be compounded in many ways. The mildest was *iuinti*, already discussed in connection with the etymology of *tesgüino*, translated by Siméon (*Diccionaire*) simply as "to be drunk." From this root are derived terms for gaiety and good humor. The next was *tlauana*, "drink much, to get moderately drunk." The final term, *xocomictia*, was to "get drunk" in the highest degree, almost literally to enter the "fruit of hell." The word for habitual drunkard, *xocomiquini*, is derived from it.

The existence of a general word for drunkenness based on *xocotl* would point to an important early utilization of the acidulous fruits in the manufacture of fermented drinks.

The naming process is inductive rather than deductive, just the reverse of that found in the case of *tesgüino*, but the implication of an early importance is quite the same. The chances are that the term was developed by the lowland Nahua, since most of the *xocotl* fruits are native to the *tierra caliente*, and that it later spread to the plateau.

94. Martínez, *Catálogo*, 82–84.

95. W. Popenoe and A. Pachano, "The Capulín Cherry," *Journal of Heredity* 13 (1922): 51–61. The authors cite Cobo to the effect that the plant was brought to Lima from Mexico at some time in the first half of the seventeenth century. The common name for the plant in Ecuador is *capulí*, practically the Nahuatl form, which also points to a colonial introduction.

96. Cortés, "Third letter to Charles V" (from Cuyoacan), May 15, 1522, *Cartas*, vol. 2, 9.

97. We cannot always be sure we are dealing with *P. capuli* or even with the genus *Prunus*, although in many cases the words "*cerezo*" or "*cerezas*" are used and in some others the accompanying description confirms the identification.

98. Ximénez, *Quatro libros*, 67: "Bread and wine are made from this fruit when one or the other fail." The bread referred to is *capultamalli*, made from cornmeal to which *capulín* juice or the ground pulp has been added.

99. Sahagún (*Historia general*, vol. 3, 226–27) gives a *capulín* list which is interesting for comparison:

(1) *Amacapulin*—The mulberry. Literally, "paper cherry." Identified by Standley (*Trees and Shrubs*, 204) as *Morus celtidifolia*.

(2) *Capulin*—"*Cereza*" (cherry).

(3) *Elocapulin*—Bigger tree than ordinary *capulín*. Very tasty fruit. *Elotl* means a green ear of corn. The derivation of the name "*elocapulin*" is uncertain.

(4) *Tlaolcapulin*—Smaller tree than *capulín*. Smaller fruit [of the size of a maize grain (from *tlaolli*, maize grain) according to Siméon (*Diccionaire*).

(5) *Xitomacapulin*—Big juicy cherries with small kernel but thick skin. *Xitomatl* is the common red tomato.

With the exception of *amacapulin*, none of the names in this list or in the list from the Totonac area have been taxonomically synonymized.

100. Martínez, *Plantas útiles*, 103.

CHAPTER 8

1. Second anonymous [witness], *in* García Icazbalceta, *Col. doc. hist. de Méx.*, vol. 2, 304, and Third anonymous [witness], ibid., vol. 2, 451. As discussed in chapter 7, note 20, the statement of the third "witness," "They make much pulque from mescal and plums," undoubtedly refers to mescal wine rather than to pulque.

In passing it might not be out of place to recall that the very name "Tahue" is suggestive of drunkenness. There seems to be no record as to the original meaning of the tribal name, but the Cora dictionary of Ortega gives "*Beodo* [drunkard]. *Tahua*" and "*Borrachera* [drunkenness]. *Tahuâeiat*" (*Vocabulario*, 11). The word appears to derive from a Uto-Aztecan root for drunkenness, of which another example is "*tlauana*" of highland Nahuatl for which Siméon gives "*boire beaucoup, s'enivrer modérément* [to drink much, to become moderately intoxicated]" (*Dictionnaire*).

2. Sauer, "Aboriginal Tribes and Languages," 6–7.

3. *Relación geográfica* for the Cora Mission *In* Biblioteca Nacional de México, MS 15-3-76.

4. I have seen these bromelias in the jungles of coastal Colima and Guerrero, and in some of the drier portions of Guatemala and Salvador. The plants prefer an *Aw* (or *Cw*) environment to *Am* or *Af.* They are related to the pineapple (*Ananas sativa*) and have a very similar growth habit, the main difference being that the central stalk bears a peduncle with separate fruit pods instead of a completely fused mass. The individual pods are the size of fat Brazil nuts but have a round rather than triangular cross section. Samples found in the markets of Guadalajara were externally bright purplish red, while others seen in Las Casas, Chiapas, were yellow with a delicate red tint. The taste in each case was the same— excessively sweet and syrupy, with a somewhat tart, lip-biting aftereffect.

5. *Relación geográfica* of 1777 for San Ignacio de Huainamota *in* Biblioteca Nacional de México.

6. *Relación geográfica* of 1579 for Tenemaztlán in *Noticias*, 324, 336, 340.

7. *Relación geográfica* of 1777 for Autlán *in* Paso y Troncoso, *Papales*, transcript in the Museo Nacional de México, part of unpublished tomo 8.

8. *Relación geográfica* of 1579 for Zapotitlán in *Noticias*, 296; *relación* of 1579 for Tuscaquesco ibid., 305

9. *Relación geográfica* of 1778 for Ystlahuacan (Ixtlahuacan) *in* Paso y Troncoso, *Papeles*, transcript in the Museo Nacional de México, part of unpublished tomo 8. The *relación geográfica* of 1789 for Tecalitan (ibid.) covers a large portion of the province of Colima; the MS fills 108 pages.

10. In June 1939, while on a trip to Ixtlahuacan in the company of Dr. Carl O. Sauer and Dr. Isabel Kelly, my attention was called to a bunch of large grapelike fruit, apple-red in color, which grew on a vine with tendrils. The fruit was one-half to three-quarters inch in diameter, had the slip skin typical of native American grapes, and bore seeds that looked like large grape seeds. It had a good flavor. The fruit was larger than that of any native American *Vitis* and is probably identifiable with *Ampelocissus acapulcensis* (see Standley, *Trees and Shrubs*, 733). At the time, we were unable to ascertain a possible native use of the fruit in the manufacture of wine, but Dr. Kelly subsequently wrote from the same vicinity that she had verified the existence of such a beverage.

11. *Relación geográfica* of 1589 for Motín *in* Paso y Troncoso, *Papeles*, transcript in the Museo Nacional de México, part of unpublished tomo 8.

CHAPTER 9

1. *Relación geográfica* for Tenemaztlán, 1579, in *Noticias*.

2. *Codex Mendoza, Codice Mendocino,* "Mexico," 36–37 ff.

3. *Relación geográfica* for Xalapa (de Guerrero), 1582, *in* Paso y Troncoso, *Papeles*, 2d series, vol. 4, 261.

4. L. Schultze-Jena, *Indiana* (Jena, 1938), vol. 3, 144.

5. *Relación geográfica* for Citlaltomague y Anecuilco, 1580, *in* Paso y Troncoso, *Papeles*, 2d series, vol. 6, 153–66.

6. To my knowledge the 1580 *relación* for Citlaltomague y Anecuilco (see note 5, above) is the only sixteenth-century reference to banana wine in Mexico, but there is not the least indication in this account that the beverage was not aboriginal. Native spokesmen answered most of the questions. The story of the banana in the southwestern lowlands of Mexico needs still to be written. It might be added in passing that the Purificación (Jalisco) *relación* of 1585 (*in* Paso y Troncoso, *Papeles*, 2d series) mentions the use of bread from bananas as one of the

main foods of the natives, and that the Ameca *relación* of 1579 (*in* Paso y Troncoso, *Papeles*, 2d series) records the occurrence of bananas in the canyons of neighboring hills.

7. Although the words "*pulque*" and "*mague*" are used in the 1580 *relación* for Citlaltomague y Anecuilco (*in* Paso y Troncoso, *Papeles*, 2d series, vol. 6, 153–66), it is unlikely that real pulque is involved. More likely, mescal wine is meant, possibly mescal brandy. The area is far removed from the continuous pulque region and in too low a location. Cacao was grown here, and cacao and pulque were nowhere else found together in the same area.

8. *Relación geográfica* for Yhualapa, 1582, *in* Paso y Troncoso, *Papeles*, 2d series, vol. 4, 265.

9. Spelled variously *xocoyolle, xocollole, socollole, xoutyulle,* etc.

10. Hernandez, *Nova plantarvm.*

11. *In* Paso y Troncoso, *Papeles* (transcript in the Museo Nacional de México, part of unpublished tomo 8).

12. *Relación geográfica* for Chinantla, 1579, *in* Paso y Troncoso, *Papeles*, 2d series, vol. 4, 62.

13. *In* Paso y Troncoso, *Papeles*, 2d series, vol. 4, 224. The official spelling of the town is now Mazatlán and the name of the tribe, Mazatec. The dropping of the 't' is most unfortunate; the name thereby loses its geographic validity. "Matzatlán" in Nahuatl means "place of pineapples" (*matzatli*, "pineapple"; -*tlan*, "place of"), and the appellation is very apt since the area has been known since pre-Columbian times for the abundance and good quality of this fruit. Even today, great quantities of large, sweet pineapples are grown for export. "Mazatlán" also means "place of deer" (*mazatl*, "deer"). While the latter meaning might be entirely appropriate, it is not the derivation given in the 1579 *relación*.

14. *In* Paso y Troncoso, *Papeles* (transcript in the Museo Nacional, Mexico, part of the unpublished tomo 8).

15. Palm-stem wine in the New World presents some intricate problems:

(1) The method widely prevalent in recent times of felling the palms is not likely to be aboriginal since it is doubtful whether the Indians had tools sufficiently sharp and strong to chop down mature palm trees. Steel machetes are used today. Hence palm wine, if made aboriginally in the New World, must have been derived from sap drawn from living, upright palms, and the Chiapas procedures just described are probably post-Conquest.

(2) If coyol-palm wine was an aboriginal trait in Mexico, one would expect to find native words for the wine. In the lowland Nahua areas, one might expect the name "*coyuloctli*" to be used, but to my knowledge this word was never so much as coined by the Nahua. The Navarro report mentions "*pulque de coyol*" (*in* Orozco y Berra, *Apéndice*), but this terminology is obviously post-Conquest. The most common term for coyol wine in Chiapas is "*taberna*," a Spanish word that was used also in Africa and the Canary Islands. There is, however, a significant variation in usage. According to the information in G. A. de Herrera (*Agricultura general* [Madrid, 1777]), the word "*taberna*" is applied in the Canary Islands to the palm that is tapped—an entirely logical use of the word—while the sap is called "*garapo*." The Chiapas usage is arbitrary rather than logical, and it, therefore, seems likely that the Old World usage is earlier. It is entirely possible that blacks may have played a part in the imperfect transfer of nomenclature, and it is also entirely possible that they played an important role in the extension of the method of palm-stem tapping, if, indeed, they did not introduce the whole technique into the New World.

(3) With one exception, the earliest chroniclers in America do not mention palm-stem wine. The palm wine recorded by Oviedo is a wine from the fruit of the peach palm, *pejiballe*

(*Guilielma utilis*), which is a very different matter. (See note 37, below.) He says (*Historia general*, vol. 1, 334): "There are other palms . . . which they call "*pixabay*" and which have clusters like grapes that are eaten and made into a good wine that is in excellent supply." Cieza de León mentions the same palm-fruit wine, but also states that the palmito of this palm was used for food around Antioquia (Colombia) (*Crónica*, 364). The one exception regarding the use of palm-stem wine comes from the earliest report of Central America. Ferdinand Columbus, in his account of his father's fourth voyage, makes the following statement in connection with the first Spanish visit to Veragua (the northwestern coast of Panama) in 1503:

> They also make another sort of wine of certain trees like palms; and I believe they are that kind, but they are smooth and have such prickles on the trunk as thorns. From the pith of this palm, which is like palmitoes squeez'd, they draw a juice, whereof they make wine, boiling with it water and spice; and this they make great account of (*Churchill's Voyages* [London, 1732], vol. 2, 591).

The Spanish version of 1749 (Madrid), translated from the Italian, shows certain deviations, and may be nearer to the original account:

> They make another wine from certain trees that have spines on the trunk as large as those of the porcupine. From the heart of these palms, like the palmettos, is squeezed and pressed out a large amount of what the wine is made from, and it is boiled in water and made like other wines of its kind. The wine is considered very good and valuable (ibid., 112).

The description of spines on the trunk would apply to *Acrocomia vinifera*, the best wine palm of Central America.

Offhand it would seem that this statement from the account of the first expedition to Central America would prove conclusively the indigenous character of the trait of palm-stem tapping, no matter how similar the technique may be to the African process. But there is still room for doubt. Culture historians have largely ignored the unequivocal statements of early chroniclers that blacks were found in Panama by Balboa's party. Thus, Peter Martyr, in his *De orbe novo: Third decade*, written in 1516 (p. 286), writes:

> The Spaniards found negro slaves in this province. They only live in a region one day's march from Quarequa and they are fierce and cruel. It is thought that negro pirates of Ethiopia established themselves after the wreck of their ships in the mountains. The natives of Quarequa carry on incessant war with these negroes.

"Ethiopia" in the early sixteenth century did not have the specific regional connotation that it bears today.

López de Gómara's account adds some significant details:

> When Balboa arrived in Quarequa, he did not find negro slaves for the Señor. He asked where he could find them, and it could not be said or explained more than that there were men of that color nearby, with whom they waged customary war. These could be the first negroes to be seen in the Indies, and also it was believed that more had not been seen (*Historia general de las Indias*, 2d ed. [Madrid, 1922], vol. 1, 114).

On page 162 he calls these people "*negros como de Guinea*." They could hardly have been dark-skinned Indians or Polynesians or Melanesians, since the Spaniards were well acquainted with blacks from Africa and identified them as such. The simplest and best explanation may be that they were descendants of people from Africa who had come relatively recently to this part of the New World and who had passed along to their Indian neighbors certain African traits, including that of palm-stem tapping.

16. The origin of the term "chicha" is still obscure. The word is widely used east and south of Tehuántepec and is applied to a great variety of alcoholic drinks. To the north, it is used very seldom. Leo Wiener has made a partial study of the word, and he may be right in his opinion that it stems from the Old World (*Africa*, vol.2, 114 ff.). The first use of the word thus far found in the literature is dated 1516 and refers to Castilla del Oro: "The wives of the cacique always drank chicha, made by their own hands" (Col. doc. inéd . . . ultramar, vol. 2, 485).

17. S. G. Morley and G. W. Brainerd, *The Ancient Maya*, 4th ed., revised by R. J. Sharer (Stanford, 1983), 483, 493.

18. D. de Landa, *Relación de las cosas de Yucatán*, 7th ed. (Mexico, 1938); T. López de Médel, *De los tres elementos . . . acerca de las Occidentales Indias . . .*, Academia de la Historia, Muñoz Col., 42 (Madrid). Photographic copy at the University of California Library, Berkeley.

19. Published *in* Col. doc. inéd . . . ultramar, vols. 11 and 13. About 50 *relaciones* are published in these two volumes, but the aggregate information in them is rather less than that in the other *relaciones* of Mexico. The reasons are twofold: (1) Maya culture and the natural environment were strikingly uniform over large areas, and (2) a large proportion of these accounts were written in whole or in part by the same man, Gaspar Antonio Chi. He was an educated Maya, a descendant of the old ruling family of Chi (or Xiu), who enjoyed the confidence and respect of the natives and the Spaniards alike (see Frans Blom, "Gaspar Antonio Chi, Interpreter," *American Anthropologist*, n.s., 30 [1928]: 250–62). Gaspar Antonio was obviously a very competent individual to have contributed to the writing of these *relaciones*, but it is also obvious that one of the main purposes of the *relaciones*, the recording of as much information as possible of regional importance, was defeated by his prolix authorship.

20. K Sapper, "*Bienenhaltung and Bienenzucht in Mittelamerika und Mexico*," "*Beiträge zur Bienenzucht in Mittelamerika und Mexico*," *Ibero-Amerikanisches Archiv* 9 (1935): 183–98; 11 (1938): 497–505.

21. Morley and Brainerd, *Ancient Maya*, 35, 493, 494.

22. *Relación geográfica* for Dohot and Tetzimin (in *Col. doc. inéd . . . ultramar*, vol. 13, 207). Gaspar Antonio had nothing to do with the writing of this account; it is due to Giraldo Díaz Dalpuche, who, according to his own testimony, married one of the nieces of Moteçuma, the Aztec ruler.

23. In *Col. doc. inéd . . . ultramar*, vol. 11, 49.

24. Ibid., vol. 11, 90, 97.

25. A. M. Tozzer, *A Comparative Study of the Mayas and the Lacandones* (New York, 1907), 124.

26. Used, for example, in J. P. Perez's *Diccionario de la lengua Maya* (Mérida, 1866–1877). On page 19 he writes: "*Balché*: a tree with whose dry bark the Indians ferment the cane juice, resulting in a liquor called "*pitarrilla*." See also S. Mendez, "The Maya Indians of Yucatan in 1861," *Indian Notes and Monographs* 9 (1921): 151: "Their usual beverage is palles *pitarrilla*, consisting of the bark of a plant called *balché*."

27. E. H. Blair and J. A. Robertson (eds. and anns.), *The Philippine Islands 1493–1803* (Cleveland, 1903–1909), vol. 3, 55–56. Mirandaola writes:

> They [the inhabitants of the Philippines] have wines of many kinds: brandy, made from palm-wine which is obtained from the cocoa-nut palm, and from the wild nipa palm; *pitarillos*, which are the wines made from rice, millet, and borona; and other wines, made from sugar cane.

28. J. Soustelle, *La culture materielle des Indiens Lacandons*, Université de Paris, Faculté des Lettres (Société des Americanistes, 1937), 37.

29. A. M. Tozzer, "A Spanish Manuscript Letter on the Lacandones, in the Archives of the Indies at Seville," *Proc. Int. Cong. Amer.* (London, 1913), vol. 1, 504.

30. See G. A. de Herrera, *Agricultura general: Que trata de la labranza del campo y sus particularidedes* . . . (Madrid, 1777). The latex of this tree is the commercial source of chicle, used in the manufacture of chewing gum. The plant is indigenous in the territory of the Lacandón. The fruit is more or less round, generally two or three inches in diameter, and contains a sweet, brownish pulp of rather insipid taste.

31. T. Gage, *A New Survey of the West Indies*, 3d ed. (London, 1677), 323.

32. F. W. McBryde, "Native Economy of Southwestern Guatemala and Its Natural Background," Ph.D. diss., University of California, Berkeley, 1941. This use of "*chicha*" is reminiscent of the "*ciruela borrachera*" mentioned for southern Jalisco.

33. MS, Archivo del Gobierno, Guatemala, A3.4, *Embriaguez*, 1784-.35.137-.2378. This extensive report is for the whole Audiencia and contains information on as far south as Nicoya. It evidently fulfilled the same functions as the 1784 Navarro report for Mexico (*in* Orozco y Berra, *Apéndice*).

34. For example, *in* Fuentes y Guzmán, *Recordación Florida*, vol. 2, 164: "A felled trunk . . . of the coyols, in the center of its length they opened a hollow like a small canoe; and when that was done, and all of the fluid of that cavity was collected, it became an excellent white wine, and its taste was highly favored." Opening the trunk in the middle of its length represents still another variation in method from those cited previously.

35. MS, Archivo del Govierno, Guatemala, A3.4, *Embriaguez*.

36. Oviedo, *Historia general*, vol. 1, 307, vol. 4, 104.

37. The fact that Oviedo in the 1530s does not list coyol palm wine, while Cistue in the 1770s finds it to be one of the two most important beverages (MS, Archivo del Gobierno, Guatemala, A3.4, *Embriaguez*), is excellent evidence for our thesis that the wide distribution of this beverage is a colonial phenomenon.

38. Ibid.

39. In Biblioteca Nacional de México, "*Relacion de los Religiosos . . . de Guat^a segun . . . que se ordena por R^l Cedula de 21 de Mayo de 1717—*," MS 3/84(4), f. 28.

40. Gage, *New Survey*.

41. Columbus, *Churchill's Voyages*, vol. 2, 606.

42. E. Conzemius, "Ethnographical Notes on the Black Carib (Garif)," *American Anthropologist*, n.s., 30 (1928): 183–205. The author states that these people were resettled in Central America by the British government. Their original home was St. Vincent, one of the Windward Islands. It should be mentioned in passing that they brought with them the manufacture of manioc beer, which reaches its northernmost limit in the New World in Central America.

43. E. Conzemius, *Ethnographical Survey of the Miskito and Sumu Indians of Honduras*, Bureau of American Ethnology Bulletin no. 106 (1932), 98–101.

44. Ibid.

45. Ibid.

46. Ibid.

47. F. Martínez Landero, "*Los Taoajkas ó Sumos del Patuca y Wampú*," *Revista del Archivo y de la Biblioteca Nacional de Honduras*, vol. 14, 301–3, 363–64, 431–34, 496, 496, 559–60, 627–28, 691–92; vol. 15, 39–41, 102–4.

48. H. Pittier, *Apuntaciones ethnológicas sobre los Indios Bribri*, Serie Ethnológica del Museo Nacional (San José, Costa Rica), no. 1 (1938), 15.

49. M. M. de Peralta, *Costa-Rica, Nicaragua, y Panamá* (Madrid, 1883), 522.

50. Oviedo, *Historia general*, vol. 1, 283; vol. 3, 136, 142.

51. E. Nordenskiöld (in collaboration with H. Wassén and R.P. Kantule), *An Historical and Ethnological Survey of the Cuna Indians*, Comparative Ethnological Studies (Göteborgs Museum), no. 10 (1938), 250.

Appendix B

1. Gage, *New Survey*.

2. Aguillar (*Cuapatli ó madera*) states in connection with the pulque root *quauhpatli* that the pulque of the Valley of Oaxaca, which is made with the root, keeps its "fluidity" (i.e., low viscosity) for three to five days, while the pulque of the Mesa Central, which is made without the root, becomes viscous in about two days. This may indicate, provided other factors are constant, that the pulque root has a selective effect on the activities of the microorganisms responsible for the viscous fermentation.

3. An excellent discussion of the nature of these substances, together with some general statements as to their history, distribution, and physiological activity, is to be found in L. F. Fieser, *The Chemistry of Natural Products Related to Phenanthune* (New York, 1936), 256–316.

4. I am indebted to Professor Gordon Mackinney, Department of Fruit Products, College of Agriculture, University of California, for directing these tests.

5. Standley, *Trees and Shrubs*, 385–86.

6. Gage, *New Survey*.

7. Ibid.

8. Ibid.

9. Ibid.

Bibliography

Academia de la Historia (Madrid). *Relación geográfica* for Chilchota, Michoacán, October 15, 1579. MS 12-18-3, no. 16, doc. 6, 22 ff. Photographic copy at the University of California, Berkeley.

Aguilar, A. L. "*El cuapatli ó madera del pulque.*" *El México Antiguo* 2 (1924): 14–19.

Albornoz, R. de. Letter to Charles V, December 15, 1525. *In* J. García Icazbalcéta. *Col. doc. hist. de Méx.*, vol. 1, 488. Mexico, 1858–1866.

Alegre, F. X. *Historia de la Compañia de Jesús en Nueva España.* Bustamente edition. 3 vols. Mexico, 1841.

Alexander, H. B. *Latin American Mythology.* Boston, 1920.

Anghiera, Pietro Martire d'. *See* Martyr, P.

Archivo de Instrumentos Públicos de Jalisco, Ramo de Tierras y Aguas. Report of Daualos y Toledo in 1616. *In* Libro 1, no. 3. Guadalajara.

Archivo General de la Nación, Ramo de Ordenanzas. Vol. 2, 207v–8. Mexico City.

Archivo del Gobierno, Guatemala. MS A3.4. "*Embriaguez.*" 1784-.35.137-.2378.

Arias y Saavedra. *Informe* (1673). *In* A. Santoscoy, *Nayarit.* Colección de documentos inéditos, históricos y etnográfica, 7-35, 25. Guadalajara, 1899.

Arlegui, J. *Chronica de la Provincia de N.S.P.S., Francisco de Zacatecas.* Mexico, 1737.

Baegert, J. *Nachrichten von der Amerikanischen Halbinsel Californien.* Mannheim, 1772.

Barrera, J. de la. [Report on prohibition, 1692.] Museo Nacional de México. E.B.T. 2.336, ff 48–53v.

Bauhin, C. *Teatri Botanici.* Basel, 1623

Beals, R. "The Comparative Ethnology of Northern Mexico before 1750. *Ibero-Americana* 2 (1932): 159.

Beaumont, P. *Crónica de Michoacan* (18th century). Publicaciones del Archivo General de la Nación. 3 vols. Mexico City, 1932.

Bennett, W. C., and R. M. Zingg. *The Tarahumara: An Indian Tribe of Northern Mexico.* Chicago, 1935.

Berger, A. *Die Agaven.* Jena, 1915.

Biblioteca Nacional de México. "*Carta escrita de Nachitos p' el Cavallero Macartij ad" Angel Marios y Navarrete en 17 de 9bre de 1763.*" 1 f.-v. Mexico City.

＿＿＿. "*Costumbres de los Indios Apaches (Lipanes).*" 4 ff. Legajo 99, no. 66 (filing system prior to 1939). Mexico City.

_____. Letter of Estteuan Lorenzo to the viceroy, December 10, 1790. Legajo 93, no. 3, 102–18v. ff.

_____. *Relación geográfica* for the Cora Mission, Jesús María y José, of 1777. MS 15-3-76.

_____. *Relación geográfica* for San Miguel el Grande, Obispado de Michoacán, of August 30, 1777. MS 15-3-76.

_____. *Relación geográfica* for San Ygnacio de Huainamota, 1777.

_____. *Relación geográfica* for Yscatun (Tecual), 1777.

_____. "*Relacion de los Religiosos . . . de Guath͡e segun . . . que se ordena por R͡l Cedula de 21 de Mayo de 1717—*." MS 3/84(4).

_____. Report of Pedro Fages to Bucareli of November 14, 1775. Legajo 53, no. 37.

Blair, E. H., and J. A. Robertson, eds. and anns. *The Philippine Islands, 1493–1803.* 55 vols. Cleveland, 1903–1909.

Blom, F. "Gaspar Antonio Chi, Interpreter. *American Anthropologist* n.s., 30 (1928): 250–62.

Bourke, J. G. "The Folk-Foods of the Rio Grande Valley and of Northern Mexico." *Journal of American Folklore* 8 (1895): 41–71.

Bravo, H. *Las cactáceas de México.* Mexico, 1937.

Bravo, J. "*Razon de la entrada al Puerto de la Paz, Conquista de la Nación Guaycura, y fundación de la Misión de Nuestra Señora del Pilar en California, año de 1720.*" MS, Biblioteca Nacional de México, legajo 53, no. 19°. Mexico City.

Britton, N. L., and G. N. Rose. "Cactaceae." *In* P. C. Standley, *Trees and Shrubs of Mexico,* 855–1012. Washington, D.C., 1924.

_____. *The Cactaceae.* 4 vols. Washington, D.C., 1919–1923.

Buckley, S, B. *Second Annual Report of the Geological and Agricultural Survey of Texas.* Houston, 1876.

Bulnes, F. *El pulque e studio científico.* Mexico, 1909.

Carbajal, A. J. "*La fermentación racional del pulque.*" Sociedad Científica "Antonio Alzate" Memoria no. 32, 219–66. Mexico City, 1912.

Cardenas, J. de. *Primeros parte de los problemas y secretos marauillosos de las Indias.* 1st ed. Mexico, 1591; 2d ed. Mexico, Imp. del Museo n. de arqueología historia, y etnológia, 1913.

Casas, G. de las. *Libro intitulado Arte para criar seda desde que se rebive una semilla hasta sacar otra.* Granada, 1581.

Castetter, E. F., and W. H. Bell. *The Aboriginal Utilization of the Tall Cacti in the American Southwest.* University of New Mexico Bulletin no. 307. Albuquerque, 1937.

Castetter, E. F., W. H. Bell, and A. R. Grove. *The Early Utilization and the Distribution of Agave in the American Southwest.* University of New Mexico Bulletin no. 335. Albuquerque, 1938.

Chabot, F. C. *Excerpts from the Memorias for the History of the Province of Texas.* Morfi, 1932.

Cieza de León, P. de. *Crónica del Perú.* Madrid, c1922.

Clavigero, F. J. *Historia antigua de México y de su conquista.* Mexico, 1844.

Codex Mendoza, Codice Mendocino. "Mexico." Phototypic edition. 148 pl. 1925.

Col. doc. inéd. . . . hist. de España. *Relación de las ceremonias y ritos, polación y gobierno de los indios de la provincia de Mechoacan.* Madrid, 1842–1895, vol. 53.

Col. doc. inéd . . . ultramar. *Relaciones geográficas.* For:

the Maya, 1579, vols. 11 and 13

Hocaba and Cotuto y Tibolon, vol. 11

Mérida, 1579, Vol. 11

Pánuco, 1609, vol. 9

Tanteyuc (Tantoyuca), vol. 9

the Yucatan, the Dohot and Tetzimin (author, Giraldo Díaz Dalpuche), vol. 13

_____. [Report of chicha at Castilla del Oro, 1516], vol. 2, 485.

Columbus, F. *Churchill's Voyages*. Vol. 2. London, 1732; Spanish version, Madrid, 1749.

Conzemius, E. "Ethnographical Notes on the Black Carib (Garif)." *American Anthropologist*, n.s., 30 (1928): 183–205.

_____. *Ethnographical Survey of the Miskito and Sumu Indians of Honduras*. Smithsonian Institution, Bureau of American Ethnology Bulletin no. 106. Washington, D.C., 1932.

Cortés, H. Fourth letter to Charles V, October 15, 1524. In *Cartas de relación de la conquista de Méjico*, vol. 2, 81. Calpé edition. Madrid, 1922. Also in *Col. doc. hist. de Méx*, edited by J. García Icazbalcéta, vol. 1, 475.

_____. Second letter to Charles V, October 30, 1520. In *Cartas de relación de la conquista de Méjico*, vol. 1, 99. Calpé edition. Madrid, 1922.

_____. Third letter to Charles V, May 15, 1522. In *Cartas de relación de la conquista de Méjico*, vol. 2, 9. Calpé edition. Madrid, 1922.

Costa Alvarez, A. *El ultimo diccionario de la academia*. La Plata, 1925.

Crist, R. E. "Some Geographic Aspects of the Manufacture of Mezcal." *Scientific Monthly* 50 (March 1940): 224-236.

Cushing, F. H. *Zuñi Breadstuff*. Indian Notes and Monographs no. 8. New York, 1920.

Dávila Garibi, I. *Breves apuntes acerca de los Chimalhuacanos*. Guadalajara, 1927.

Diguet, L. *Les cactacées utiles du Mexique*. Paris, 1928.

_____. "*Étude sur le maguey de tequila*." *Revue de Cultures Coloniales* 10 (1902): 294–97, 321–26, 357–61.

_____. *La sierra du Nayarit et ses indigènes*. *Nouvelles Archives des Missions Scientifiques et Litteraires* 9 (1899): 571–630.

Fages, P. Report to Bucareli of November 14, 1775. *In* Biblioteca Nacional de México. Legajo 53, no. 37. Mexico City. Also: Priestley, H. I., trans. *A Historical, Political, and Natural Description of California by Pedro Fages, Solder of Spain*. Berkeley, 1937.

Fernandez Tagle, G. *Estudio de las vitaminas y de la fermentación viscose en el pulque*. Mexico City, Universidad de México, 1931.

Fieser, F. L. *The Chemistry of Natural Products Related to Phenanthrene*. New York, 1936.

Figueroa, G. de. *Puntos de anua de estos diez años que he asistido en este partido de San Pablo (1662)*. *In* Documentos para la historia de Méjico, 4th series. Vol. 3, 217-21. Mexico, 1857.

Forde, C. D. *Ethnography of the Yuma Indians*. Berkeley, 1931.

Fuentes y Guzmán, F. A. *Recordación florida: Discurso historial*. . . . Biblioteca "Goathemala" de la Sociedad de Geográfica e Historia, vol. 6 in 3 vols. Guatemala, 1932–33.

Gage, T. *A New Survey of the West Indies*. 3d ed. London, 1677.

García, G., and C. Pereyra. *Doc. inéd. ó muy raros hist. Méj.* Vol. 25, 37–38, 42–45.

García Icazbalceta, J. *Obras de d. J. García Icazbalceta*. 10 vols. Mexico City, 1896–1899.

_____, ed. First anonymous [witness]. In *Col. doc. hist. de Méx.*, vol. 2. Mexico, 1858–1866.

_____. Hernán Cortéz's fourth letter to Charles V, October 15, 1524. In *Col. doc. hist. de Méx.*, vol. 1, 475. Mexico, 1858–1866.

_____. *Relación de Texcoco*, 1582. In *Nueva colección de documentos para la historia de México*. 5 vols. Mexico, 1886–1892.

_____. Rodrigo de Albornoz's letter to Charles V, December 15, 1525. In *Col. doc. hist. de Méx.*, vol. 1, 488. Mexico, 1858–1866.

_____. Second anonymous [witness]. In *Col. doc. hist. de Méx.*, vol. 2, 304. Mexico, 1858–1866.

_____. Third anonymous [witness]. In *Col. doc. hist. de Méx.*, vol. 2, 451. Mexico, 1858–1866.

Garcilaso de la Vega. *Primera parte de los comentarios reales.* Lisbon, 1609; Madrid, 1723.

Gates, W., trans. *The De la Cruz–Badiano Aztec Herbal of 1552.* The Maya Society Publication no. 23. Baltimore, 1939.

Genin, A. *La cerveza entre los antiguos mexicanos y en la actualidad.* Mexico, 1924.

Gentry, H. S. *The Warihio Indians of Sonora-Chihuahua: An Ethnographic Survey.* Smithsonian Institution, Bureau of American Ethnology Anthropological Paper no. 65. Washington, D.C., 1963.

Gifford, E. W. *The Kamia of Imperial Valley.* Smithsonian Institution, Bureau of American Ethnology Bulletin no. 97. Washington, D.C., 1931.

Gonzalez, E. *"Análisis del Tejuino."* MS in the Escuela de Farmacia, Universidad de Guadalajara, Mexico.

Griffiths, D., and R. F. Hare. *Prickly Pear and Other Cacti as Food for Stock.* New Mexico Agricultural Experiment Station Bulletin no. 60. Albuquerque, November 1906.

Hare, R. F., and D. Griffiths. *The Tunas as a Food for Man.* New Mexico Agricultural Experiment Station Bulletin no. 64. Albuquerque, April 1907.

Hare, R. F., S. R. Mitchell, and A. P. Bjerregaard. *Denatured Alcohol from Tunas and Other Sources.* New Mexico Agricultural Experiment Station Bulletin no. 72. Albuquerque, August 1909.

Hartwich, Carl. *Die Menschlichen Genussmittel, ihre herkunft, arbreitung, geschichte, anwendung, bestandteile und wirkung.* Leipzig, 1911.

Havard, V. *Drink Plants of the North American Indians.* Torrey Botanical Club Bulletin 23 (1896): 33–46.

Hernández, F. *Historia natural de Nueva España.* 2 vols. Mexico City, 1959–1967.

_____. *Nova plantarvm, animalivm et mineralivm Mexicanorvm.* Rome ed., 1651; Madrid ed., 1790; F. Ximénez, trans. 2d ed. Morelia, Mexico, 1838.

Herrera, G. A. de. *Agricultura general: Que trata de la labranza del campo y sus particularidades. . . .* Madrid, 1777.

Hodge, F. W., ed. *Handbook of American Indians North of Mexico.* 2 vols. Washington, D.C., 1907–1910.

Hough, W. *The Hopi Indians.* Cedar Rapids, Iowa, 1915.

Hrdlička, A. "Method of Preparing Texvino among the White River Apaches." *American Anthropologist*, n.s., 6 (1904): 190–91.

_____. "Notes on the Indians of Sonora, Mexico." *American Anthropologist*, n.s., 6 (1904): 51–89.

_____. *Physiological and Medical Observations among the Indians of Southwestern United States and Northern Mexico.* Smithsonian Institution, Bureau of American Ethnology Bulletin no. 34. Washington, D.C., 1908.

_____. "The Region of the Ancient 'Chichimecs,' with Notes on the Tepecano and the Ruin of La Quemada, Mexico." *American Anthropologist*, n.s., 5 (1903): 385–440.

Jimenez Moreno, W. *Mapa lingüistico de Norte y Centro-América.* Mexico, 1936.

Kniffen, F. B. *Lower California Studies. III: The Primitive Cultural Landscape of the Colorado Delta.* University of California Publications in Geography 5, no. 2, 43–66. Berkeley, 1931.

Köppen, W. P., and R. Geiger. *Handbuch der Klimatalogie*. Berlin, Gebrüder Borntraeger, 1930.

Kroeber, A. L. *Handbook of the Indians of California*. Smithsonian Institution, Bureau of American Ethnology Bulletin no. 78. Washington, D.C., 1925.

_____. *The Seri*. Southwest Museum Papers no. 6. Los Angeles, 1931.

_____. *Walapai Ethnography*. American Anthropological Association Memoir 42. Menasha, 1935.

La Barre, W. "Native American Beers." *American Anthropologist*, n.s., 40 (1938): 224–34.

_____. *The Peyote Cult*. Yale University Publications in Anthropology no. 19. New Haven, 1938.

Landa, D. de. *Relación de las cosas de Yucatán*. 7th ed. Mérida, 1938.

Latcham, R. E. *La agricultura precolombiana en Chile y los paises vacinos*. Santiago, 1936.

León, A. de. "Testimony." *In* G. García and C. Pereyra, *Doc. inéd. ó muy raros hist. Méj*. Vol. 25, 38, 42–45.

Lindner, P. "*Das Geheimnis um Soma*. . . ." *Forschungen und Fortschritte* 9 (1933): 65–66.

_____. *Mikroskopische und biologische Betriebskontrolle in dem Gärungsgewerbe, sechste neuarbeitete Auflage*. Berlin, 1930.

Lobato, J. G. *Estudio quimico-industrial de los varios productos del maguey mexicana*. Mexico, 1884.

López de Gómara, F. *Historia de México*. 2d ed. Anvers, 1554.

_____, ed. *Historia general de las Indias*. Vol. 1. Madrid, 1922.

López de Médel, T. *De los tres elementos . . . acerca de las Occidentales Indias*. . . . Academia de la Historia, Muñoz Col. vol. 42. Madrid. Photographic copy at the University of California Library, Berkeley.

Lumholtz, C. *New Trails in Mexico*. New York, 1912.

_____. *Unknown Mexico: A Record of Five Years' Exploration*. 2 vols. New York, 1902.

Macias and Rodriguez. Tuxpaneca, 210.

Martínez, M. *Catálogo de nombres vulgares y científicos de plantas mexicanas*. Mexico, 1937.

_____. *Plantas útiles de México*. 2d ed. Mexico, 1936.

Martínez Gracida, M. *Historia antigua de la Chontalpa Oaxaqueña*. Sociedad Científica "Antonio Alzate" Memoria no. 30, 29–104, 225–325. Mexico City, 1910.

Martínez Landero, F. "*Los Taoajkas ó Sumos del Patuca y Wampú*," *Revista del Archivo y de la Biblioteca Nacional de Honduras* 14 (1934): 301–3, 363–64, 431–34, 496, 559–60, 627–28, 691–92; 15 (1935): 39–41, 102–4.

Martyr, P. [Anghiera, Pietro Martire d'.] *De orbe novo: Third Decade*. 1516.

McBryde, F. W. "Native Economy of Southwestern Guatemala and its Natural Background." Ph.D. diss., University of California, Berkeley, 1941.

McGee, W J. *The Seri Indians*. Smithsonian Institution, Bureau of American Ethnology 17th Annual Report. Washington, D.C., 1898.

Maurizio, A. *Geschichte der gegorenen Getränke*. Berlin, 1933.

Memorias para la historia de Sinaloa. *Carta Anua* (1593). MS 227, Mex., pp. 26, 86. University of California, Berkeley, Bancroft Library.

Mendez, S. "The Maya Indians of Yucatan in 1861." *Indian Notes and Monographs* 9 (1921): 137–95.

Mendieta Huerta, E. "*La economía de los pueblos indígenas huastecos de San Luis Potosí*." *Revista Mexicana de Sociología* 2 (1939): 57–68.

Mendoza, G. "*Sendechó.*" *Boletín de la Sociedad Mexicana de Geografía y Estadística*, 2d epoca, 2 (1870): 25–28.

Molina, A. de. *Vocabulario en lengua mexicana y castellana.* . . . Mexico, 1571.

Mota y Escobar, A. de la. *Descripción geográphica de los reynos de Galicia, Vizcaya, y Leon* [written between 1602 and 1605]. Mexico, 1930.

Motolinía (de Benavente), T. *Historia de los indios de la Nueva España.* D. Sánchez García edition. Barcelona, 1914.

_____. *Memoriales.* Mexico, 1903.

[Nentvig, J.]. *Rudo ensayo, by an unknown Jesuit padre, 1763.* Trans. by Eusebio Guitéras. 1951.

Nordenskiöld E. (H. Wassén and R.P. Kantule, collabs.). *An Historical and Ethnological Survey of the Cuna Indians.* Göteborg Museum, Comparative Ethnological Studies no. 10. 1938.

Noticias varias de Nueva Galicia. *Relación geográfica* for:
Tenemaztlán, 1579.
Tequaltiche, 1584.
Tuscaquesco, 1579.
Zapotitlán, 1579.

Núñez de Haro y Peralta, A. "*Carta al juez de bebidas prohibidas,*" July 3, 1787. MS 318. Biblioteca Nacional de México, Mexico City.

Orozco y Berra, M. *Apéndice al diccionario universal de historia y de geografía.* Tomo 1 (8 of the work). Mexico, 1855.

_____. *Historia antigua de la conquista de México.* vol, 1. Mexico, 1880.

Orozco y Jiménez, F. *Col. doc. hist. inéd.* . . . *Arzobispo, Guadalajara.* Vol. 5, no. 1. Guadalupe, January 1, 1926.

Ortega, J. de. *Apostólicos afánes de la Compañia de Jesus.* Barcelona, 1754.

_____. *Vocabulario en lengua Castellana y Cora.* Mexico, 1732.

Oviedo y Valdes, G. F. de. *Historia general y natural de las Indias, islas y tierra del mar oceano.* 4 vols. Madrid, 1851–1852.

Palacios, E. *El alcoholismo en el problema indígena de México. Boletín de la Sociedad Mutualista Médico-Farmaceutica de Guadalajara* no. 9, 261–80. Guadalajara, 1937.

Paso y Troncoso, F. del. *Relaciones geográficas.* In *Papeles de Nueva España.* 2d series: *Geografía y estadística.* For:
Ameca, 1579.
Atlatlauca y Malinaltepec, 1579, vol. 6; 1580, vol. 5.
Chiconauhtla, January 4, 1580, vol. 6.
Chinantla, 1579, vol. 4.
Chilapa, 1582, vol. 4.
Citlaltomagua [Guerrero] y Anecuilco, 1580, vol. 6.
Cuauhquilpan, 1581, vol. 6.
Cuicatlán, Oaxaca, 1579, vol. 4; 1580 ?, vol. 4.
Guaxilotitlán, 1581, vol. 4.
Ichcateopan, 1580, vol. 6.
Jalapa, Veracruz, 1580, vol. 5.
Mazatlán, 1579, vol. 4.
Miaquatlán, 1580, vol. 4.

Pánuco, 1579, vol. 4; 1580, vol. 6.

Papaloticpac, 1579, vol. 6.

Purificación (Jalisco), 1585.

Tepeaca, 1580, vol. 5.

Tepoztlán, 1579, vol. 4; 1580, vol. 6.

Texcatepec, 1579, vol. 6.

Xalapa (de Guerrero), 1582, vol. 4.

Xalapa de la Veracruz [Jalapa], October 20, 1580, vol. 5.

Yhualapa, 1582, vol. 4.

Zimapan, 1579, vol. 6.

_____. Transcript of *Papeles* in Museo Nacional de México (part of the unpublished tomo 8, vols. 1 and 2). Photographic copy at the University of California Library, Berkeley.

Pópulo Gueguachic, Nueva Viscaya, December 4, 1777, legajo 4, no. 41 (author signs himself Padre Mariano).

Relación geográfica for Autlán, 1777.

Relación geográfica for Chacaltianguiz, 1777.

Relación geográfica for Chilchota, Michoacán, 1579.

Relación geográfica for Coscatlan (Coxcatlán), 1777

Relaciones geográfica for Coatlan and Guijecollani (southern Oaxaca), 1777.

Relación geográfica for Motín, 1589.

Relationes geográfica for Nuchistlán and Suchipila, 1584, vol. 1.

Relación geográfica for "Quacoman" of 1580, vol. 2.

Relación geográfica for Taltenango, 1584, vol. 1.

Relación geográfica for Tecalitan, 1789.

Relación geográfica for Ystlahuacan (Ixtlahuacan), 1778.

Patiño, C. *Vocabulario Totonaco*. Xalapa, 1907.

Payne, E. J. *History of the New World Called America*. Oxford, 1892.

Peralta, M. M. de. *Costa-Rica, Nicaragua, y Panamá*. Madrid, 1883.

Perez, J. P. *Diccionario de la lengua Maya*. Merida, 1866–1877.

Pérez, L. *Estudio sobre el maguey llamado mezcal en el Estado de Jalisco*. Guadalajara, 1887.

Pérez de Luxán, D. *Expedition into New Mexico Made by Antonio de Espejo, 1582–1583, as Revealed in the Journal of Diego Pérez de Luxán*. Trans. by George Peter Hammond and Agapito Rey. Los Angeles, 1929.

Perez de Ribas, A. *Historia de los trivmphos de nvestra Santa Fe. . . .* Madrid, 1645.

Pfefferkorn, I. *Beschreibung der Landschaft Sonora*. Cologne, 1794.

Pittier, H. *Apuntaciones ethnológicas sobre los Indios Bribri*. Serie Ethnológica del Museo Nacional no. 1. San José, Costa Rica, 1938.

Plancarte y Navarrete, F. H. *Prehistoria de México*. Tlalpam, D.F., 1923.

Ponce, A. *Viaje a Nueva España*, vol. 1, 241. Mexico, 1947.

Popenoe, W., and A. Pachano. "The Capulín Cherry." *Journal of Heredity* 13 (1922): 51–61.

Preuss, K. T. "*Der Ursprung der Religion und Kunst.*" *Globus* 87 (1905): 418.

Priestley, H. I., trans. *A Historical, Political, and Natural Description of California by Pedro Fages, Soldier of Spain*. Berkeley, 1937.

Prieto, A. *Historia, geografía y estadística del Estado de Tamaulipas*. Mexico, 1873.

Ramírez Laguna, A. *Distribución de los agaves de México*. Anales del Instituto de Biología (de la Universidad Nacional Autónoma), vol. 7. Mexico, 1936.

Redfield, R. *Tepoztlan: A Mexican Village*. Chicago, 1930.

Robelo, C. A. *Diccionario de Aztequismos*. Cuernavaca, 1904; new edition, 1912.

Roca, J., and R. Llamas. *Las vitaminas del pulque*. Anales del Instituto de Biología (de la Universidad Nacional Autónoma), vol. 9, 81–84. Mexico, 1938.

Ruiz de Alarcon, H., P. Sanchez de Aguilar, and Gonzalo de Balsalobre. *Tratado de las idolatrías, supersticiones, dioses, ritos, hechicerías y otras costumbres gentílicas de las razas aborígenes de México* (1629). *Anales del Museo Nacional de México*, 1st epoca, vol. 6, 127–223. Mexico City, 1892, 1900.

Russell, F. *The Pima Indians*. Smithsonian Institution, Bureau of American Ethnology 26th Annual Report. Washington, D.C., 1808.

Sahagún, B. de. *Historia general de las cosas de Nueva España* [*Florentine Codex*]. 5 vols. Mexico, 1938. (English-Nahuatl edition of the *Florentine Codex*, translated by C. E. Dibble and A. J. O. Andersen, published by the University of Utah Press in 12 Books, plus introductory volume.)

Sánchez y More, José Mariano (Conde dal Peñasco). *See* Zeschan Noamira, J. R.

Santa Maria, V. *Relación histórica de la Colonia del Nuevo Santander, México*. Archivo General de la Nación Publicación no. 15, 406. Mexico, 1930.

Santoscoy, A. *Nayarit. In* Colección de documentos inéditos, históricos y etnográficos, 7–35, 25. Guadalajara, 1899.

Sapper, K. "*Bienenhaltung and Bienenzucht in Mittelamerika und Mexico*"; "*Beiträge zur Bienenzucht in Mittelamerika und Mexico*." *Ibero-Amerikanisches Archiv* 9 (1935): 183–98; 11 (1938): 497–505.

Sauer, C. O. "The Distribution of Aboriginal Tribes and Languages in North-Western Mexico." *Ibero-Americana* 5 (1934): 1–90.

Sauer, C. O., and D. Brand. "Aztatlán." *Ibero-Americana* 1 (1932), 53.

Sauer, C. O., and P. Meigs. *Lower California Studies I. Site and Culture at San Fernando de Velicata*. University of California Publications in Geography, Vol. 2, No. 9: 271–302. Berkeley, 1927.

Sayles, E. B. *An Archaeologic Survey of Texas*. Medallion Papers no. 17, 134. Gila Pueblo, Globe, Arizona, 1935.

Schultze-Jena, L. "*Bei den Azteken, Mixteken, und Tlapaneken der Sierra Madre del Sur von Mexico*." In *Indiana*, vol. 3. Jena, 1938.

Segura, J. C. *El Maguey*. 4th ed. Mexico, 1901.

Seler, E. G. *Gesammelte Abhandlungen zur Amerikanischen Sprach und Altertumskunde*. 5 vols. Berlin, 1902–1923.

_____. *Die Wandskulpturen im Tempel des Pulquegottes von Tepoztlan*. Congrès International des Américanistes, 1906, vol. 2, 351–79. Quebec, 1907.

Shantz, H. L., and R. Zon. Natural Vegetation. In *Atlas of American Agriculture*, 24. Washington, D.C., 1924.

Siegel, R. K. *Intoxication: Life in Pursuit of Artificial Paradise*. New York, 1989.

Siméon, R. *Dictionnaire de la langue Nahuatl*. Paris, 1885.

Soustelle, J. *La culture materielle des Indiens Lacandons*. Université de Paris, Faculté des Lettres, Société des Americanistes, 1937.

_____. *La famille Otomi-Pami du Mexique Central*. Paris, 1937.

Spier, L. *Yuman Tribes of the Gila River*. Chicago, 1933.

_____. *Havasupai Ethnography*. New York, 1928.

Standley, P. C. *Trees and Shrubs of Mexico*. Contributions from the U.S. National Herbarium no. 23. 5 parts. Washington, D.C., 1920–1926.

Stevenson, M. C. *Ethnology of the Zuñi Indians*. Smithsonian Institution, Bureau of American Ethnology 30th Annual Report. Washington, D.C., 1915.

Tapia Zenteno, D. de. *Arte novissima de lengua mexicana*. Mexico, 1753.

_____. *Noticia de la lengua Huasteca*. Mexico, 1767.

Torres, C. F. de. *Virtudes maravillosas de pulque, medicamento universal, ô polychresto*. MS 13-8-26. Biblioteca Nacional de México, Mexico City.

Tozzer, A. M. *A Comparative Study of the Mayas and the Lacandones*. New York, 1907.

_____. "A Spanish Manuscript Letter on the Lacandones in the Archives of the Indies at Seville." Proceedings of the International Congress of Americanists, vol. 1. London, 1913.

Trelease, W. *Agave. In* P.C. Standley, *Trees and Shrubs of Mexico*. Contributions from the U.S. National Herbarium no. 23, 107–42. Washington, D.C., 1920–1926.

_____. *Agave in the West Indies*. Memoirs of the National Academy of Sciences, vol. 11. 1913.

Trimborn, H. *Quellen zur Kulturgeschichte des präkolumbischen Amerika*. Stuttgart, 1936.

Underhill, R. *The Autobiography of a Pápago Woman*. American Anthropological Association Memoir no. 46. Menasha, 1936.

Vasco de Puga. *Provisiones, cédulas, instrucciones para el gobierno de la Nueva España*, f.70. Mexico, 1563; Madrid, 1945.

Vega, G. de la. *Primera parte de los commentarios reales*. Lisbon, 1609; Madrid, 1723.

Velasco, J. F. *Noticias estadísticas de Sonora*. Mexico, 1850.

Velasco, Juan de. *Historia del Reino de Quito (1789)*, vol. 1. Quito, 1844.

Velázques, G. *Colección . . . San Luis Potosí*, vol. 1, 1–48.

Wagner, G. *Entwicklung und Verbreitung des Peyote-Kultes*. Baessler Archiv 15 (1932): 59–141.

Waugh, F. W. *Iroquois Foods and Food Preparation*. Canada Department of Mines, Geological Survey Memoir no. 86. Ottawa, 1916.

Weil, A. *The Natural Mind: An Investigation of Drugs and the High Consciousness*. Rev. ed. Boston, 1986.

Wiener, L. *Africa and the Discovery of America*. 3 vols. Philadelphia, 1920–22.

Woodward, A. The "Honey" of the Early California Indians—A Strange Ethnological Error. *The Masterkey* 12 (1938): 175–80.

Ximénez, F. *Quatro libros de la náturaleza y virtudes medicinales de las plantas y animales, de la Nueva España*. Edited by N. León. Morelia, Mexico, 1888.

Zeschan Noamira, J. R. [José Mariano Sánchez y Mora, Conde del Peñasco]. *Memoria instructiva sobre el maguey o Agave mexicano*. Mexico, 1837.

Zingg, R. M. *The Huichols: Primitive Artists*. University of Denver Contributions to Ethnography no. 1. New York, 1938.

_____. *A Reconstruction of Uto-Aztecan History*. University of Denver Contributions to Ethnography no. 2. New York, 1939.

About the Author

Compiled by Ronald F. Lockmann

Henry J. Bruman is Professor Emeritus of Geography at the University of California, Los Angeles. Born in Berlin in 1913, he moved to a small town near Brunswick, where he lived until 1922, when his family emigrated to the United States to join his maternal grandfather in Los Angeles. He attended Los Angeles city schools, graduating from Manual Arts High School in 1930. He attended California Institute of Technology and the University of California, Los Angeles, where he graduated with a degree in chemistry in 1935. He had already discovered geography as an academic discipline, taking a class the previous year at the Escuela Verano, National Autonomous University of Mexico. Completing another degree, in Geography, at UCLA, he took the advice of Ruth E. Baugh, and went north to study with the noted cultural geographer of Latin America, Carl O. Sauer, at the University of California, Berkeley, in 1936. He became Sauer's eleventh Ph.D. graduate, after completion of his dissertation in 1940. Based on his fieldwork in west-central Mexico, his work epitomized the Sauerian method of original field observation combined with utilization of key archival source materials, as well as familiarity with contemporary sources to solve problems in the evolution of landscape patterns and origins of cultural systems. The field notebooks and photographs from his travels into Mexico and adjacent Central American countries in 1937–39 formed the basis for the dissertation, "Aboriginal Drink Areas of New Spain." Partial support came from a Social Science Research Council grant.

After an initial academic position starting in 1940 at Pennsylvania State College Department of Earth Sciences for three years, he served as cultural geographer at the Smithsonian Institution under Julian Steward and was a visiting fellow at Harvard in the Department of Geology and Geography over the next two years. In 1945, he accepted an offer from his alma mater as Latin Americanist in the Geography Department, replacing George McBride. He advanced through the professorial ranks, retiring in 1983. During his career there, he published research articles, taught, traveled frequently and extensively in Latin America and Europe. He spent 1966–68 at Georg August Universität, Göttingen, West Germany, as director of the Education Abroad Program for the University of California system. The Universität appointed him to a position there—in addition to his University of California position. He has listed his professional research and teaching interests as Latin America, plant geography, the scientific exploration and settlement of the American West—especially by the pioneer naturalist-geographers and the geographical science of Alexander von Humboldt. He helped found the Map Library with University Librarian Lawrence Clark Powell. The Office of Naval Research supported his research on postwar settlement in Brazil with several graduate students. He codirected the Latin American Studies Center at UCLA. He directed the U.S. Department of State sponsored binational student exchanges with Colombia and Brazil, and, as an architect of the postwar expansion of the department, he trained numerous academics and researchers who served in professional positions around the globe.

Over the course of his career he received numerous honors and awards, including Fellow of the American Geographical Society, 1941; Fellow, American Association for the Advancement of Science, 1946; Fulbright Scholarship/Fellowship to Portugal, 1963; Alexander von Humboldt Gold Medal from the Federal Republic of Germany, 1971; 250th Anniversary Silver Medal, Georg August Universität, Göttingen, West Germany, 1978.

During the past two decades, in partial response to the austerities of his own youth, he set about systematically directing his accumulated financial resources to support educational goals of research and scholarly endeavors at UCLA, the most notable of which include the Henry J. Bruman Graduate Fellowship in Cultural-Historical Geography (1978); the Saul Winstein Chair in Chemistry (1995); the Henry J. Bruman Endowed Chair in Germanic History (1990); the Henry J. Bruman Educational Foundation Fund (1992); the Henry J. Bruman Library, Maps, and Government Information and Library System (1987); the Alexander von Humboldt Endowed Chair in Geography (1996); the H. J. Bruman Chamber Music Series, with free summer concerts, UCLA; the Los Angeles Public Library; Support for Organization of Tropical Studies; and the American Geographical Society, New York.

The Henry J. Bruman Archive resides at UCLA in the Young Research Library, Department of Special Collections and is accessible on the Online Archive of California: http://www.oac.cdlib.org/

Henry J. Bruman
Selected Bibliography

Compiled by Ronald F. Lockmann

"The Russian Investigations on Plant Genetics in Latin America and Their Bearing on Culture History." In *Handbook of Latin American Studies, 1936*, 449–58 (Cambridge, Mass., Harvard University Press, 1937).

"Aboriginal Drink Areas in New Spain," Ph.D. diss., University of California, Berkeley, Department of Geography, 1940.

Review of C. L. Lundell's "The 1936 Michigan-Carnegie Botanical Expedition to British Honduras." *Geographical Review* 31, no. 3 (July 1941): 505–6.

Review of R. Stadelman's "Maize Cultivation in Northwestern Guatemala." *Geographical Review* 31, no. 4 (October 1941): 675.

"The Sixteenth Century *Relaciones Geograficas* for Mexico." (Abstract) *Association of the American Geographers Annals* 32, no. 2 (March 1942): 105–6.

Review of F. Termer's "*Zur Geographie der Republik Guatemala; Beitrage zur Kultur- und Wirtschaftsgeographie von Mittle- und Süd-Guatemala.*" *Geographical Review* 32, no. 2 (April 1942): 338–40.

Review of J. Frenguelli's "Rasgos principales de Fitogeographia Argentina." *Geographical Review* 33, no. 1 (January 1943): 151–52.

Note on "The House of Tlaloc and Its First Publication." *Acta Americana* 1, no. 1 (January–March 1943): 147–48.

Critical summary of Antonio Vasquez de Espinosa's "Compendium and Description of the West Indies." *Acta Americana* 1, no. 1 (January–March 1943): 159–64.

Review of R. Ardissone's "*La instalacion humana en el Valle de Catamarca: Estudio anthropogeografico.*" *Geographical Review* 33, no. 3 (July 1943): 504–5.

Review of articles relating to the Western Hemisphere appearing in the *Geographical Review* 33 (July 1943); *Acta Americana* 1 (July–September 1943): 402–4.

"The Asiatic Origin of the Huichol Still." *Geographical Review* 34, no.3 (July 1944): 418–27.

"Some Observations on the Early History of the Coconut in the New World." *Acta Americana* 2, no. 3 (July–September 1944): 220–43.

Review of articles relating to the Western Hemisphere appearing in the *Geographical Review* 34, no. 1 (January 1944); *Acta Americana* 1, nos. 1 and 2 (January–June 1944): 127–30.

"Southern Brazil as a Theater of Postwar Colonization." "M" Project Report (R 112), 1945. MS copy at UCLA, Geography Department. [HJB is author of reports on pp. 83 and 352.]

"Early Coconut Culture in Western Mexico." *Hispanic American Historical Review* 25, no. 2 (May 1945): 212–23.

Review of R. Baron Castro's *"La poblacion de El Salvador: Estudio acerca de su desenvolvimiento desde le época prehispanica hasta nuestros días."* *Geographical Review* 35, no. 4 (October 1945): 686–87.

"A Further Note on Coconuts in Colima." *Hispanic American Historical Review* 27, no. 3 (August 1947): 572–73.

Review of Domingo Lazaro de Arregui's *"Descripción de la Nueva Galicia."* *Hispanic American Historical Review* 27, no. 4 (November 1947): 526–27.

Review of Walter V. Schole's "The Diego Ramirez Visita." *Hispanic American Historical Review* 27, no. 4 (November 1947): 669–70.

"The Culture History of Mexican Vanilla." *Hispanic American Historical Review* 28, no. 3 (August 1948): 360–76.

"Recent Agricultural Colonization in Brazil." *Association of American Geographers Annals* 45, no. 2 (June 1955): 171–72.

"Post-War Agricultural Colonization in Brazil." Technical Report, ONR Contract 233(03), 1958. MS copy at UCLA, Geography Department.

"Latin America." In *Military Aspects of World Political Geography*, 139–73. Maxwell Air Force Base, Alabama: Air University, 1959.

"The Caribbean and the Panama Canal." In *The Changing World: Studies in Political Geography*, edited by W. G. East and A. E. Moodie, 860–80. New York, 1960.

"Man and Nature in Mesoamerica: The Ecologic Base." In *Indian Mexico Past and Present*, edited by Betty Bell, 13–24. Los Angeles: UCLA Latin American Studies Center, 1967.

"Alexander von Humboldt & the Exploration of the American West." Los Angeles: UCLA Library, 1971. 7pp.

"In Memory of Carl Sauer." *Historical Geography* 6 (1976): 5–7.

"Sovereign California: The State's Most Plausible Alternative Scenario." In *Early California: Perception and Reality*, 1–41. Los Angeles: William Andrews Clark Memorial Library, 1981.

"Carl Sauer in Mid Career: A Personal View by One of His Students." In Martin Kenzer (Ed.), *Carl O. Sauer—Tribute*, edited by Martin Kenzer, 125–37. Corvallis: Oregon State University Press, 1987.

"The Schaffhausen Carta Marina of 1531." *Imago Mundi* 41 (1989): 124–32.

"Recollections of Carl Sauer and Research in Latin America." *Geographical Review* 86, no. 3 (July 1996): 370–76.

Index